CHUANG-TZU

*A New Selected Translation with an
Exposition of the Philosophy
of Kuo Hsiang*

BY FUNG YU-LAN

FOREIGN LANGUAGES PRESS   BEIJING

First Edition 1989
Fourth Printing 1995

Originally published by
the Commercial Press
1931

ISBN 7-119-00104-3

Published by Foreign Languages Press
24 Baiwanzhuang Road, Beijing 100037, China

Distributed by China International Book Trading Corporation
35 Chegongzhuang Xilu, Beijing 100044, China
P.O. Box 399, Beijing, China

Printed in the People's Republic of China

PUBLISHER'S NOTE

The English translation of the *Chuang-tzu* by Professor Fung Yu-lan, a distinguished contemporary Chinese philosopher, was first published in 1931 by the Commercial Press. With Professor Fung's permission the book is reprinted for the sake of interested readers abroad. Apart from changes in style and occasional changes in phraseology, Chapter Ten, "The Third Phase of Taoism: Chuang Tzu," of Professor Fung's *A Short History of Chinese Philosophy* is included as an appendix in the present edition with a view to offering readers better understanding of Chuang Tzu and his writings.

CONTENTS

CONTENTS

PREFACE

There are already several English translations of Chuang Tzu's writings in circulation. Why should we offer a new one?

In answering this question, two reasons may be given: In the first place, a translation is an interpretation or commenting. So far as the English translations of the *Chuang-tzu* are concerned, they may be good and useful from a literary or linguistic point of view. But in their interpreting the *Chuang-tzu*, they do not seem to have touched the true philosophical spirit of the author. In other words, they are successful in the literary or linguistic aspect, but not in the philosophical. Since Chuang Tzu's writings, like Plato's "Dialogues," are more a philosophical work than a literary one, it seems that a new translation, which would put more emphasis on Chuang Tzu's philosophy, is needed.

In the second place, the Ching Dynasty is famous for scholarship. Through the works of many scholars in the field of higher and textual criticism, most of the ancient books have become more readable and intelligible. The earlier English translations of the *Chuang-tzu* do not seem to have utilized the fruit of the labour of these scholars. In this respect, a new translation, which embodies the results of recent scholarship, is also needed.

William James said that every great philosopher has his vision. When one has grasped the vision, the whole system is easily understood. Crocé said somewhere that the greater a philosophical system is, the simpler the central idea. Although the present translation is limited to the first seven chapters of Chuang Tzu's writings, it is believed that it contains the main vision or idea of the author. With the Introduction, which was originally prepared in a lecture form delivered at different institutions in Peking, and an appendix that was originally written for the *Philoso-*

1

phical Review, Peking, it is hoped that something may be contributed to the right understanding of Taoism as a philosophy.

In preparing the present translation of the *Chuang-tzu*, I have consulted other translations and utilized them freely, especially that of Legge and Giles. When a rendering is correct, it is not necessary to make it different simply for the sake of difference. However, there are important terms, phrases, or passages, which are the keys to the whole chapter, of which a different rendering may give the whole chapter a different tune or colour. In such cases, I usually give a new rendering according to what I consider the right interpretation of Chuang Tzu's philosophy. This, together with the explanations and comments, may justify my calling the present translation my own. To the other translators, however, especially to Legge and Giles, I must acknowledge my obligation.

Lastly, the reader is asked to excuse me for my limited ability in expressing myself in the English language. If he should find the book not very unreadable, or that his literary taste is not seriously offended in reading it, the merit is due to the assistance of my friends, Mr. L. C. Porter, Mr. A. W. Hummel, Mr. Mi Wu, who have read the manuscript and corrected mistakes as they found them, and to whom I take this opportunity to express my deep gratitude.

Fung Yu-lan

June, 1928,
Peking

2

INTRODUCTION

In China, Taoism has been as influential as Confucianism. It was more influential than Confucianism in the time of the "Six Dynasties"; viz., from the third to the sixth centuries. It was at that time that the Taoistic classics had their best commentators. Wang Pi's "Commentaries on the *Lao-tzu*," and Kuo Hsiang's "Commentaries on the *Chuang-tzu*," for instance, have become classics themselves; I venture to say that some passages of their "Commentaries" are even more illuminating than the texts.

The sayings of Lao Tzu and the books of Chuang Tzu and Lieh Tzu are usually regarded as the earlier classics of Taoism. Lao Tzu's book is brief enough, yet in it he spoke about many things. Sometimes his meaning is not clear, and opens up many different interpretations. The authenticity of *The Book of Lieh Tzu (Lieh-tzu)* as we possess it is much questioned. A great part of the book is now regarded by most scholars as the production of the "Six Dynasties." It is only in the *Chuang-tzu* that we have a well-developed philosophy; and a great part of that book, especially the "inner chapters," is usually considered genuine. There are also side branches of Taoism, the ultramaterialism and hedonism of Yang Chu, for instance. But Chuang Tzu's philosophy represents the main current of the Taoistic teaching. His book, with Kuo Hsiang's "Commentaries," is the most important literature of Taoism.

THE GENERAL VIEWPOINT AND THE SIGNIFICANCE OF TAOISM

Before discussing Taoism in detail, it is better for us to get familiar first with its general viewpoint. William James divided philosophers according to their temperament into two classes — the "tough-minded" and the "tender-minded." The "tough-minded" philosophers reduced mind to matter, the "higher" to the "lower"; according to them, the world is materialistic (at least nonspiritualistic), mechanistic, and deterministic. Man is alien to the world, in which there is no God, no immortality, no freedom. On the other hand, the "tender-minded" philosophers reduced matter to mind, the "lower" to the "higher." According to them, the world is spiritualistic, in which there is God, immortality, and freedom; and man, though insignificant he may appear to be, is inwardly connected with the whole. These are really the two points of view to see the world. Science takes the one point of view, religion, the other; the one is more congenial to intellect, the other, to feeling. Because the two viewpoints are different, science and religion are always in conflict. And how to reconcile this conflict has become a problem in philosophy.

In the history of philosophy, generally speaking, there were mainly two ways to reconcile these two points of view. Some philosophers (Kant, for instance) said that science is valid only in the phenomenal world; beyond the phenomenal, there is the noumenal world, which is not governed by the laws of science, and is the place for God, immortality, and freedom. James, Bergson, generally speaking, both took this view. We may call it the pragmatic (in the broad sense of the word) point of view. Other philosophers (Spinoza, for instance) fully accepted the naturalistic conception of the universe, but in their system, by a peculiar combination, there is still place for God, immortality, and freedom; man is still one with the universe, if only he can "see things under the form of eternity." The so-called new realism in contemporary philosophy seems also to take this view. We may call this the neorealistic point of view. As we shall see, Taoism also took this view. Some people said that Taoism is naturalistic and scientific, while others said that it is mystic and religious. In fact, it is both.

Among the Taoistic classics, Chuang Tzu's book is not only instructive but also interesting. Chuang Tzu was not only a philosopher but also a poet. His philosophy is like that of Spinoza; his style is like that of Plato. He expounded the laborious, abstract principles of Spinoza with concrete illustrations and poetic expression. His genius is both philosophical and literary.

TAO AND TE

Tao and *Te* are two important conceptions of Taoism. According to Taoism, *Tao*, or the Way, the Truth, is everywhere. In Chuang Tzu's book, a story reads:

> Tung Kuo Tzu asked Chuang Tzu: "Where is the so-called *Tao*?" Chuang Tzu said: "Everywhere." The former said: "Specify an instance of it." "It is in the ant." "How can *Tao* be anything so low?" "It is in the panic grass." "How can it still be lower?" "It is in the earthenware tile." "How can it still be lower?" "It is in excrement." To this Tung Kuo Tzu made no reply. Chuang Tzu said: "Your question does not touch the fundamentals of *Tao*. You should not specify any particular thing. There is not a single thing without *Tao*.... There are three terms: complete, all-embracing, and the whole. These three names are different, but denote the same reality; all refer to the one thing."[1]

This passage shows that *Tao* is not something transcending the world. It is in the world. It is everywhere. It is the whole.

The whole of what? The whole of the spontaneity or naturalness of the world. In Chuang Tzu's book, Chapter II, a person named Nan Kuo Tzu Chi is telling the story of the music of man, the music of earth, and the music of nature. But after the description of the music of earth (the noise of the wind), he stopped. Then Tzu Chi was asked by Yen Cheng Tzu Yu: "The music of earth is the noise of the wind; the music of man is the sound produced by musical instruments; but what is the music of nature?" Then Nan Kuo Tzu Chi replied: "The types of the noise are extremely different, yet they all produce themselves. Could there be any other agency that excites them?" Every noise spontaneously produces itself; this spontaneity is the music of nature. In the same way, every thing in the world spontaneous-

---

1 *Chuang-tzu*, Ch. XXII.

ly produces itself. The totality of the spontaneity of all things is *Tao*.

Because *Tao* is the total spontaneity of all things, so it can do everything by doing nothing. As Lao Tzu said, it is "producing without possession"; and Chuang Tzu said:

> O, my master! O, my master! He turns all things into pieces, yet he is not just. His blessing reaches all generations, yet he is not benevolent. He is more ancient than the most antique, yet is not old. He carves and fashions all forms, yet is not skillful. [1]

Passages like these seem to be paradoxical enough. But they are not. *Tao* is the total spontaneity of all things, and not something transcending the world. Everything spontaneously just is what it is and does what it does. So *Tao* is doing nothing. But from another standpoint what everything spontaneously is and does is also the works of *Tao*, since *Tao* is the total spontaneity of all things. *Tao*, therefore, can "do everything by doing nothing."

Taoists often said that *Tao* is "nothing," because it is not something transcending the world. Yet this "nothing" is not equal to zero, since it is the total spontaneity of all things.

Thus, by insisting that everything produces itself, Taoism destroyed the popular, or, in some instances, religious, conception of God, who is looked upon as the Creator. In this respect, Taoism is naturalistic. Yet, since there is the total spontaneity of all things, there is still unity of the world, which may also be called God, if one is pleased to call it.

Next we come to the conception of *Te*, or virtue. Lao Tzu said: "*Tao* produces a thing; *Te* maintains it." [2] Chuang Tzu said: "That which things get in order to live is called *Te*." [3] So *Te* is what an individual thing receives from *Tao*. The total spontaneity of all things is *Tao*. The spontaneity that an individual thing receives from *Tao* is *Te*. As some commentator said,

---

1 *Id.*, Ch. VI.
2 *Tao Te Ching*, 51.
3 *Chuang-tzu*, Ch. XII.

8

the relation between *Te* and *Tao* is just like that between the water in river or lake, and water in general.

THE THEORY OF LETTING ALONE

Everything has its own *Te*, or virtue. Everything has its own proper nature. Everything is happy, if it is allowed to be in accordance with its own nature. In Chuang Tzu's book, Chapter I, a story was told concerning the difference between the large fish and the small bird. Though there is a great difference between these two, yet both of them are happy, so far as they both act according to their own nature. Every modification of nature is the cause of pain and suffering. Chuang Tzu said:

> The duck's legs are short, but if we try to lengthen them, the duck will feel pain. The crane's legs are long, but if we try to cut off a portion of them, the crane will feel grief. We are not to amputate what is by nature long, nor to lengthen what is by nature short. [1]

Yet in the world, most people try to modify the nature of things. Their intention may be good. But what they consider to be good may not be considered good by others. In Chuang Tzu's book, Chapter XVIII, he told a story about the treatment of a bird by the Prince of Lu. There was a peculiar bird, newly arrived in Lu. The prince welcomed it with his state carriage, and put it in the temple. He played before it the best music, and served it with the best dinner. But the bird was frightened, was very sad, and not able to drink and eat. After three days, it died. "This is to treat a bird like a man, not as a bird." This is to impose one's own idea of good upon others. This is an example of the tragedies of our world. Taoism opposes institutions, rules, laws, and government, because all these are to impose one idea of good (if it is good) upon the infinite variety of things. So the best way to govern the world is not to govern it. As Chuang Tzu said:

---

1 *Id.*, Ch. VIII.

Let your mind make excursions in the pure simplicity. Identify yourself with the nondistinction. Follow the nature of things, and admit no personal opinion. Then the world will be in peace.[1]

THE ART OF LIVING

The theory of letting-alone is not only a political philosophy; it can also be applied as an art of living. In the human world, in the relations between man and man, we are always in a place of safety, if we will let everything do what it is fit to do, while we ourselves maintain the appearance of inferiority, ignorance, and humbleness. In Chuang Tzu's book, Chapter IV, after a description of the appearance of a most awkward man, Chuang Tzu said:

If this man, who is awkward in his bodily appearance, was still able to cultivate his body and complete his term of life, how much more may he do, who is awkward in his virtue?

And Kuo Hsiang said:

The perfect man has no utility to other things; but all things have utility to themselves; so the perfect man lets everything have its own achievement and name, but he himself is mingled with things without any distinction. Therefore, he is free from the harms of the human world, and always receives the real benefit. This is the man who is awkward in his virtue.

In dealing with other men and other things, we should let them alone without interfering with them; in dealing with ourselves, we should also let the different bodily functions alone without interfering with them. Kuo Hsiang said:

The feet can walk; let them walk. The hands can hold; let them hold. Hear what is heard by your ears; see what is seen by your eyes. Let your knowledge stop at what you do not know; let your ability stop at what you cannot do. Use what is naturally useful; do what you spontaneously can do. Act according to your will

1 *Id.*, Ch. VII.

10

within the limit of your nature, but have nothing to do with what is beyond it. This is the most easy matter of nonaction. When you are in accordance with the principle of nonaction, your life cannot but be perfect. Life in perfection is nothing but happiness. Happiness is the perfection of life, and need no external thing to be added to life. [1]

This is the Taoistic theory of the cultivation of life.

EQUALITY OF THINGS AND OPINIONS

What by nature is, is good. Chuang Tzu said:

> If a man sleeps in a damp place, he will have a pain in his loins, and half his body will be as if it were dead; but will it be so with an eel? If he be at the top of a tree, he will be frightened and all in a tremble; but will it be so with a monkey? Among these three, who knows the right way of habitation? [2]

The truth is that they are equally right and their ways of habitation are equally good. In the same way, although there is an infinite number of differences between things in different aspects, yet all are right and good. So are the different opinions in the human world. In Chuang Tzu's book, the chapter "On The Equality of Things" began with the interesting story of the different noises of the wind, the "music of earth," as was mentioned above. All these different noises, different ways of blowing, are equally good. The different human opinions are like the different noises of wind, like what Chuang Tzu called the singing of birds. They together constitute what we may call the "music of man"; they are equally right and good. The sages just amuse themselves with these variety of opinions, but do not quarrel with them. They simply stand at the "centre of the circle," as Chuang Tzu called it, to meet the infinite varieties. They let the different opinions alone, and they themselves transcend

1 *Comments to Chapter IV.*
2 *Chuang-tzu*, Ch. II.

11

them. This is what Chuang Tzu called "to take two courses at once." [1]

LIFE AND DEATH

So in the universe, nothing can be said to be superior to others; nor one form of existence can be said to be superior to another. In life we assume one form of existence. Death simply means that we have to give up this form of existence and to assume another. If this form is good, there is no reason to suppose that the others are not. As Chuang Tzu said:

> To have attained the human form is a source of joy. But in the process of evolution, there is an infinite number of other forms that are equally good. What incomparable blessing it is to undergo these countless transformations! [2]

In the same chapter, a story was told about Tzu Yu, who was going to die. His friend asked him: "Do you dislike to die?" Then Tzu Yu said: "No, why should I? If my left arm would be transformed into a cock, I should be watching with it the time of the night. If my right arm would be changed into a crossbow, I should then be looking for a bird to bring down and roast. If my rump bone would be transformed into a wheel, and my spirit into a horse, I should then be mounting it, and would not change it for another steed."
To those who feel too much sorrow for death, Chuang Tzu said:

> This is to violate the principle of nature and to increase the emotion of man, forgetting what we have received from nature. This suffering is called by the ancients the penalty of violating the principle of nature. When the master [he was speaking of Lao Tzu] came, it was because he had the occasion to be born; when he went, he simply followed the natural courses. Those who are quiet at the proper occasion, and who follow the course of nature, cannot be moved by

---

1 *Ibid.*
2 *Id.*, Ch. VI.

12

human emotions. These men are regarded by the ancients as having been released by God from suspension. [1]

What Chuang Tzu called suspension is what Spinoza called the human bondage. In Chuang Tzu's book, Chapter V, a man named the Toeless spoke of Confucius as being in bondage. Then Lao Tzu said: "Why did you not simply lead him to see that life and death are one, and that the right and the wrong are the same, so freeing him from his handcuffs and fetters?" The knowledge of seeing this is the means to transcend human bondage and to attain freedom.

IMMORTALITY

Chuang Tzu said: "Life is the composition of matter; death is the decomposition of it." [2]
There is no immortality in the ordinary sense of the word. In this respect, Taoism is again naturalistic. Yet there is another way to see the matter. Chuang Tzu said:

If we see things from the viewpoint of their difference, even liver and gall are as far from each other as Chu from Yueh. If we see things from the viewpoint of their sameness, all things are one. [3]

All the things are one; all forms of existence are one. If we see this fact, we know that death is equal to life, change is equal to eternity. Chuang Tzu said:

Grass-eating animals do not dislike to change their pasture; creatures born in water do not dislike to change their water. These minor modifications have no effect on the general uniformity, and therefore cannot affect the emotion of these creatures. Now the universe is the unity of all things. If we attain this unity and identify ourselves with it, then the members of our own body are but so much dust and dirt, while death and life, end and beginning, are but as the succession

---

1 *Id.*, Ch. III.
2 *Id.*, Ch. XXII.
3 *Id.*, Ch. V.

of day and night, which cannot disturb our inner peace; and how much less shall we be troubled by the worldly gain and loss, good luck or ill luck![1]

In another place, Chuang Tzu said:

> A boat may be hidden in a creek; a net may be hidden in a lake; these may be said to be safe enough. But at midnight a strong man may come and carry them away on his back. The ignorant do not see that no matter how well you conceal things, smaller ones in larger ones, there will always be a chance for them to escape. But if you conceal universe in the universe, there will be no room left for it to escape. This is the great truth of things.[2]

This shows that if we identify ourselves with the universe, we can never be lost. If we can see all things as one, and identify ourselves with the one, then, through all the changes of the world, our existence will eternally endure. Our existence is like fire; though the present fuel is consumed, the fire is transmitted, and we know not when it comes to an end.[3] This is a conception of immortality without the presupposition of a nonnaturalistic universe.

PURE EXPERIENCE

To know the identification of individual with the whole is one thing; to experience it is another. How can we actually identify ourselves with the universe? With the state of pure experience, is the answer. Pure experience is the experience in which we have no intellectual knowledge, in which we take simply the immediate presentation, "the *that* in short (for until we have decided *what* it is, it must be a mere *that*)," as William James said. We simply take "the *that* at its face value, neither more nor less; and taking it at its face value means, first of all, to take it just as we feel it, and not to confuse ourselves with abstract talk about

---

1 *Id.*, Ch. XXI.
2 *Id.*, Ch. VI.
3 *Id.*, Ch. III.

it,"[1] Taoism disparages knowledge, because knowledge makes distinctions, while pure experience excludes it. So Chuang Tzu said:

> The knowledge of the ancients is perfect. How perfect? At first, they did not yet know that there were things (they had experience, but no intellectual knowledge). This is the most perfect knowledge; nothing can be added. Next they knew that there were things, but they did not yet make distinctions between them. Next they made distinctions between them, but they did not yet pass judgments upon them. When judgments were passed, *Tao* was destroyed. With the destruction of *Tao*, individual preferences came into being.[2]

In the same chapter, Chuang Tzu said:

> There are some who have knowledge of beginning. There are some who have no knowledge of beginning. There are some who have no knowledge of the fact that they have no knowledge of beginning. There are some who have knowledge of being. There are some who have knowledge of nothing. There are some who have no knowledge of nothing. There are some who have no knowledge of the fact that they have no knowledge of nothing.

When there is no knowledge, there is no distinction, at least epistemologically. "So a beam and a pillar are identical; so are ugliness and beauty, greatness, wickedness, perverseness, and strangeness."[3] Thus in the state of pure experience, what is known as the union of the individual with the whole is reached. In this state there is an unbroken flux of experience, but the experiencer does not know it. He does not know that there are things, to say nothing of making distinctions between them. There is no separation of things, to say nothing of the distinction between subject and object, between the "me" and the "non-me." So in this state of experience, there is nothing but the one, the whole.

---

1 James, *Essays in Radical Empiricism*, pp. 13, 48.
2 *Chuang-tzu*, Ch. II.
3 *Ibid.*

ACTIVITY AND TRANQUILLITY

In the state of pure experience, the perfect man responds, but without knowledge. In Chuang Tzu's book, Chapter VI, he gave a description of the "true man," which reads:

> The true man of old slept without dreaming and awaked without anxiety. He ate without discrimination and breathed deep breaths. . . . He knew neither to love life, nor to hate death. Living, he experienced no elation; dying, he offered no resistance; unconsciously he went, unconsciously he came, that is all.

The mind of the perfect man is compared with still water, an empty room, and a mirror. Chuang Tzu said:

> The mind of the perfect man is like a mirror. It does not move with things, nor does it anticipate them. It responds to things, but does not retain them. Therefore, he is able to deal successfully with things, but is not affected. [1]

Therefore the perfect man is both tranquil and active. In the perfect man tranquillity and activity unite. In the same chapter, a story was used to illustrate the different aspects of the perfect man. There are four aspects: (1) tranquillity, (2) activity, (3) the balance of tranquillity and activity, (4) tranquillity in activity. And Kuo Hsiang said:

> When the perfect man is active, he is like heaven; when tranquil, he is like earth. When he is doing something, he is like flowing water. When he is doing nothing, he is like a silent abyss. Though there is a difference between the flowing water and the silent abyss, between the movement of heaven and the immovability of earth, yet all these are as they are naturally, not artificially. . . . The perfect man responds to the external things with no conscious mind, but is mysteriously coinciding with the nature of things. He goes up and down with evolution and according to the change of the world. So he can be the master of things and is following time without end.

----

1 *Id.*, Ch. VII

16

This aspect of the Taoistic teaching was much developed later in Neo-Confucianism.

ABSOLUTE FREEDOM

The perfect man, who is in identity with the universe and "goes up and down with evolution," is absolutely free. The happiness of the finite things is limited, since they have to depend upon something in order to be happy. For instance, if we find happiness only in life, we will lose it in death. If we are happy only in honour, we will not be happy in disgrace. But the perfect man is absolutely free, because he has transcended all distinctions and is happy in any form of existence. The transformation of life and death is to him but as the succession of day and night, and cannot affect him, to say nothing of the worldly gain and loss, good luck and ill luck. In speaking about Lieh Tzu, who could ride on the wind, Chuang Tzu said:

> Though he was able to dispense with walking, there is still something which he had to depend upon (that is, the wind). But if one chariots on the normality of the universe, and rides on the transformation of the six elements, and thus makes excursion in the infinite, what has one to depend upon?[1]

And Kuo Hsiang said:

> To chariot on the normality of the universe is to follow the nature of things. To ride on the transformation of the six elements is to make excursion in the road of change and evolution. If one is going on like this, where can one get the end? One will chariot on whatever one meets; what will one have to depend upon? This is the happiness and freedom of the perfect man, who unites his own self with its other.

The perfect man identifies himself with the universe, and follows the nature of things. So Chuang Tzu said: "The perfect man

---

1 *Id.*, Ch. I.

has no self; the spiritual man has no achievement; the sage has no name." [1] They have no achievement and no name, because they let everything do its own work and have its own name.

"A FREE MAN'S WORSHIP"

The perfect man is he who has "the intellectual love of God," to use an expression of Spinoza. The philosophy of Taoism and that of Spinoza are so much in agreement that one passage, which was written for an introduction to the latter, may be quoted here to illustrate the former. It reads:

> The intellectual love of God is a devotion purged of all fear, of all vain regrets and even vainer hopes. The wild and angry emotions of sorrow and pain leave the strong and noble heart of man like the tidal waves leave the scattered rocks of the shore. . . . The free man is born neither to weep nor to laugh, but to view with calm and steadfast mind the eternal nature of things.
>
> To know the eternal is the immortality we enjoy. But to know the eternal we must forget about ourselves. We must cease to be consumed by a cancerous anxiety to endure in time and be permanent in space. In the order of nature our own particular lives are of no especial importance. And unless we recognize this, we are necessarily doomed to a miserable fate. We must recognize that our mere selves can never give us ultimate fulfillment or blessedness of soul. Only by losing ourselves in nature or God can we escape the wretchedness of finitude and find the final completion and salvation of our lives. This, the free man understands. He knows how insignificant he is in the order of nature. But he also knows that if only he can lose himself in nature or God, then, in his own insignificant particularity, the eternal and infinite order of nature can be displayed. For in the finite is the infinite expressed, and in the temporal, the eternal. [2]

This attitude towards the universe is the same as is expounded by Russell. He said:

---

1 *Ibid.*
2 Joseph Ratner, *The Philosophy of Spinoza*, "Introduction," P. lxix.

18

To take into the inmost shrine of the soul the irresistible forces whose puppets we seem to be — death and change, the irrevocableness of the past, and the powerlessness of man before the blind hurry of the universe from vanity to vanity — to feel these things and know them is to conquer them. . . .

The life of man, viewed outwardly, is but a small thing in comparison with the forces of nature. The slave is doomed to worship time and fate and death, because they are greater than anything he finds in himself, and because all his thoughts are of things which they devour. But, great as they are, to think of them greatly, to feel their passionless splendour, is greater still. And such thought makes us free men; we no longer bow before the inevitable in Oriental subjection, but we absorb it, and make it a part of ourselves. To abandon the struggle for private happiness, to expel all eagerness of temporary desire, to burn with passion for eternal things — this is emancipation, and this is the free man's worship. And this liberation is effected by a contemplation of fate, for fate itself is subdued by the mind, which leaves nothing to be purged by the purifying fire of time. [1]

This seeming passivity of Taoism is certainly not "Oriental subjection." It "is emancipation," it "is the free man's worship."

CONCLUDING REMARKS

These are the main points of Taoistic philosophy. Government, laws, institutions, and all things artificial, were opposed by Taoism, because it thought that every modification of nature is the cause of pain and suffering. Intellectual knowledge is also despised, because it makes distinctions and thus destroys the mysterious whole. In Taoism, there is an idealization of the instinctive activity of primitive people, of children, of birds and beasts. In Taoism, there are arguments for the negation of civilization and intellectual knowledge, for the restoration of primitivity and instinct. No doubt there is truth in the argument. But it seems that Taoism did not notice that it is the restoration that is significant. Hegel said that the old man may utter the same creed as the child, but for him "it is pregnant with the sig-

---

1 Bertrand Russell, *Mysticism and Logic and Other Essays*, p. 55.

nificance of a lifetime." [1] "The harmoniousness of childhood is the gift from the hand of nature. The second harmony must spring from the labour and culture of the spirit." [2] Primitivity and instinctiveness emphasized by Taoism in fact should be that of the "second harmony." With the analysis of the nature of human opinions, Chuang Tzu reached the conclusion that human opinions are just like the noises of the wind. With the analysis of the nature of things, Chuang Tzu reached the conclusion that the alternation of life and death is just like the succession of day and night. These conclusions were reached as the result of intellectual hard work and not *a priori* statements. Again, the pure experience expounded in the second chapter of Chuang Tzu's book is not exactly the pure experience of a child; the absolute freedom described in the first chapter is not exactly the freedom of the small bird and the large fish. These are pure experience and freedom with self-consciousness. These are not "the gift from the hand of nature," but "the labour and culture of the spirit." But Taoism did not make clear this point.

It may be said, however, that in Taoism the ideal state for self-cultivation is not the same as that for political and social reform. In other words, the ideal state to be attained by the philosopher-king is not the same as that to be attained by his subjects. He must have great wisdom, and his wisdom guides the people to remain as children, as birds, and beasts. The "second harmony" is for the philosopher to attain to, the "first harmony" is for the common people to remain in. This seems to be the position of Taoism, though there is no explicit statement in Taoistic literature.

But for the individual, there are certainly the "first" and the "second harmony." Most of us have had the "first harmony"; and there are some, though very few, who have attained to the "second harmony." But for the human race as a whole, or for the universe as a whole, we are not sure whether there was the "first harmony" and whether there will be the "second harmony," or not. So far as we are informed by history, past and

1 *The Logic of Hegel*, Wallace's translation, p. 373.
2 *Id.*, p.55.

20

present, we cannot see how we can get along without any law, morality, institution, and government. But with the teaching of Taoism, we may know that these artificial things, necessary as they may be, are, nevertheless, evils — the less of them, the better.

At any rate, it seems that Taoism was able to give us a conception of the universe, which is at once both mystical and naturalistic, and a conception of life, which is at once both Stoic and Epicurean. The general tendency of Taoism seems to be harmonious (at least not in direct opposition) both with religion and with science, and congenial both to feeling and to intellect.

CHAPTER I
THE HAPPY EXCURSION

"Although the great is different from the small, yet if they all indulge themselves in the sphere of self-enjoyment, then all things are following their own nature and doing according to their own capacity; all are what they ought to be and equally happy. There is no room for the distinction of superior and inferior." — *Kuo Hsiang*.

In the Northern Ocean there is a fish, by the name of *kun* (鯤), which is many thousand li in size. This fish metamorphoses into a bird by the name of *peng* (鵬), whose back is many thousand li in breadth. When the bird rouses itself and flies, its wings obscure the sky like clouds.

"The general idea of Chuang Tzu is to show the happy excursion, the indulgence in the way of nonaction and self-enjoyment. He, therefore, told the story of the extremely great and the extremely small, in order to illustrate the fitness of the nature of things." — *Kuo Hsiang*.

When this bird moves itself in the sea, it is preparing to start for the Southern Ocean, the Celestial Lake.

"The *peng* cannot move itself, unless in the ocean. The air cannot bear its wings, unless it reaches to a height of ninety thousand li. The *peng* is not doing so for the sake of curiosity. It does so, simply because large things must live in a large place; and in a large place, large things must be produced. Reason is naturally so. There is no mistake to fear; there is no room for conscious purpose." — *Kuo Hsiang*.

A man named Chi Hsieh[1] (齊諧), who recorded novel occurrences, said: "When the *peng* is moving to the Southern Ocean, it flaps along the water for three thousand li. Then it ascends on a whirlwind up to a height of ninety thousand li, for a flight of six months' duration."

---

1 Chi Hsieh is the name of a person, not that of a book, according to Yu Yueh.

"Since the wings are large, they are difficult to move. They must mount upon a whirlwind in order to get up, and must get to the height of ninety thousand li, in order to be supported by the air. Since the *peng* has such wings, how can it suddenly get up, and get down at the height of tens of feet? The *peng* has its own way of doing things, because of necessity, not because it likes to. The large bird flies with a duration of half a year and stops at the Celestial Lake. The small bird flies with a duration of half a morning and stops at the trees. If we compare their ability, there is a difference. But what each does is proper to its own nature; in this they are the same." — *Kuo Hsiang.*

There is the wandering air; there are the motes; there are living things that blow one against another with their breath.

"This is to illustrate that the action of the *peng* is just as natural as the movement of the wandering air, or the motes." — *Kuo Ching-fan.*

We do not know whether the blueness of the sky is its original colour, or is simply caused by its infinite height. When the *peng* sees the earth from above, just as we see the sky from below, it will stop rising and begin to fly to the south. Without sufficient depth, the water would not be able to float a large boat. Upset a cup of water into a small hole, and a mustard seed will be the boat. Try to float the cup, and it will stick, because the water is shallow and the vessel is large. Without sufficient density, the wind would not be able to support the large wings. Therefore, when the *peng* ascends to the height of ninety thousand li, the wind is all beneath it. Then, with the blue sky above, and no obstacle on the way, it mounts upon the wind and starts for the south.

"These are to show that the reason why the *peng* must fly at such a height is that it has large wings. What the small needs is not great; what the great needs cannot be small. Therefore, natural reason has its fittest course; things have their proper limitation. All things can do something, and can equally succeed. If one misses the fundamentals of forgetting life, but struggles for what is beyond the most proper, doing not in accordance with one's natural ability, acting not with

26

one's genuine feeling, one will certainly get into trouble, no matter whether one is with the large wings that cloud the sky, or simply with a sudden flight like the small bird." — *Kuo Hsiang*.

A cicada and a young dove laugh at the *peng*, saying: "When we make an effort, we fly up to the trees. Sometimes, not able to reach, we fall to the ground midway. What is the use of going up ninety thousand li in order to start for the south?"

"If there is satisfaction to their nature, the *peng* has nothing to be proud of in comparison with the small bird, and the small bird has no desire for the Celestial Lake. Therefore, though there is a difference between the great and the small, their happiness is the same." — *Kuo Hsiang*.

He who goes to the grassy suburbs, taking enough food for three meals with him, comes back with his stomach as full as when he started. But he who travels a hundred li must grind flour enough for a night's halt. And he who travels a thousand li must supply himself with provisions for three months.

"The further one goes, the more food one has to prepare. In the same way, the larger the wings are, the more air is needed." — *Kuo Hsiang*.

What do th ese two creatures know?

Since the cicada and the dove are small, they know nothing about the large. — *Translator*.

Small knowledge is not to be compared with the great nor a short life to a long one. How do we know that this is so? The morning mushroom knows not the end and the beginning of a month. The chrysalis knows not the alternation of spring and autumn. These are instances of short life. In the south of the Chu state, there is Ming-ling （冥靈）, whose spring is five hundred years, and whose autumn is equally long. In high antiquity, there was Ta-chun （大椿），[1] whose spring was eight hundred years, and whose autumn was equally long. Peng Tsu[2] was the one specially renowned until the present day for his length of life. If all men were to match him, would they not be miserable?

"There is a great difference between small and great knowledge, short and long life. If there are things to be regretted, this certainly is one. The fact that people do not regret this is for the reason that in the nature of things there are proper limitations. If we know for things there is a proper limit, beyond which nothing can be desired, in the world there would be nothing to be regretted. The great things usually do not crave for the small, but the small usually do long for the great. Therefore, Chuang Tzu showed the proper limitations of the great and the small, which are not to be excelled by merely craving and longing. If people knew this, they would not be troubled with craving and longing. Regret is born in trouble. If there is no trouble, there would be no regret. If there is no regret, life would certainly be in peace." — *Kuo Hsiang.*

In the question put by Tang[3] to Chi, there was a similar statement: "In the barren north, there is a sea, the Celestial Lake. In it there is a fish, several thousand li in breadth, and no one knows how many li in length. Its name is the *kun*. There is also a bird, named the *peng*, with a back like Mount Tai, and wings like clouds across the sky. Upon a whirlwind it soars up to a height of ninety thousand li. Beyond the clouds and atmosphere, with the blue sky above it, it then directs its flight to the south, and thus proceeds to the ocean there.

"A quail laughs at it, saying: 'Where is that bird going? I spring up with a bound, and when I have reached not more than a few yards I come down again. I just fly about among the brushwood and the bushes. This is also the perfection of flying.

---

1 According to some commentators, both Ming-ling and Ta-chun are names of trees. According to others, these are names of persons.

2 Peng Tsu is said to be a man of the Shang Dynasty, who lived as long as eight hundred years.

3 Tang was a king of the Shang Dynasty.

Where is that bird going?'" This is the difference between the great and the small.

There are some men whose knowledge is sufficient for the duties of some office. There are some men whose conduct will secure unity in some district. There are some men whose virtue befits him for a ruler. There are some men whose ability[1] wins credit in the country. In their opinion of themselves, they are just like what is mentioned above.

> "All are like the birds enjoying themselves each in its own sphere."
> — *Kuo Hsiang.*

Yet Sung Yung Tzu[2] laughed at it.

> "He laughed, because he cannot equalize the differences." —
> *Kuo Hsiang.*

If the whole world should admire him, he would not be encouraged thereby, nor if the whole world should blame him would he thereby be discouraged. He held fast the difference between the internal and the external. He marked distinctly the boundary of honour and disgrace. This was the best of him. In the world such a man is rare, yet there is still something which he did not establish.

> "He only knew that he himself was right, but not that everything is right." — *Kuo Hsiang.*

Lieh Tzu could ride upon the wind and pursue his way, in a refreshing and good manner, returning after fifteen days. Among those who attained happiness, such a man is rare. Yet, although he was able to dispense with walking, he still had to depend upon something.

> That is, the wind. — *Tr.*

---

1 Reading 而 as 能, according to Kuo Ching-fan.
2 This philosopher was mentioned by Mencius as Sung Ching; by Hsun Tzu as Sung Niu.

But suppose there is one who chariots on the normality of the universe, rides on the transformation of the six elements, and thus makes excursion into the infinite, what has he to depend upon?

> "The universe is the general name of all things. The universe has all things for its contents; and the norm of all things must be the natural. What is spontaneously so, not made to be so, is the natural. The *peng* can fly in the high place, the quail in the low. The Ta-chun can live for a long time, the mushroom a short one. All these capacities are natural, not made or learned. They are not made to be so, but are naturally so; thus they are normal. Therefore, to chariot on the normality of the universe is to follow the nature of things. To ride upon the transformation of the six elements is to make excursion in the road of change and evolution. If one is going on like this, where can one reach the end? If one will chariot on whatever one meets, what will one have to depend upon? This is the happiness and freedom of the perfect man who unites his own self with its other. If one has to depend upon something, one cannot be happy, unless one gets hold of the thing which one depends upon. Although Lieh Tzu could pursue his way in such a fine manner, he still had to depend upon the wind, and the *peng* was even more dependent. Only he who ignores the distinction between things and follows the great evolution can be really independent and always free." — *Kuo Hsiang.*

Therefore, it is said that the perfect man has no self; the spiritual man has no achievement; the true sage has no name.

> "Everything has its proper nature. The nature of everything has its proper limitation. The difference among things is just like that between small and great knowledge, short and long life. ... All believe in their own sphere, and none is intrinsically superior to others. After giving different illustrations, Chuang Tzu concluded with the independent man who forgets his own self and its other, and ignores all the differences. All things enjoy themselves in different spheres, but the independent man has neither achievement nor name. Therefore, he who unites the great and the small is one who ignores the distinction of the great and the small. If one insists on the distinction, the *peng*, the cicada, the small officer, and Lieh Tzu riding on the wind — all are troublesome things. He who equalizes life and death is one who ignores the distinction of life and death. If one insists on the distinc-

30

tion, Ta-chun, the chrysalis, Peng Tzu, and the morning mushroom, all suffer early death. Therefore, he who makes excursion in the nondistinction of the great and the small has no limitation. He who ignores the distinction of life and death, has no terminal. Those whose happiness is attached within the finite sphere will certainly have limitation. Though they are allowed to make excursion, they are not able to be independent." — *Kuo Hsiang.*

If things enjoy themselves only in their finite spheres, their enjoyment must also be finite. For instance, if one enjoys only in life, he would suffer in death. If one enjoys only in power, he would suffer at the loss of it. The "independent man" transcends the finite. He "hides the universe in the universe," as mentioned in Chapter VI. He thus becomes infinite, and so is his happiness. "The perfect man has no self," because he has transcended the finite and identified himself with the universe. "The spiritual man has no achievement," because he follows the nature of things and lets everything enjoy itself. "The true sage has no name," because his virtue is perfect; every name is a determination, a limitation. — *Tr.*

Yao [1] wished to resign as the ruler of the empire in Hsu Yu's [2] favour, saying: "If, when the sun and moon have come forth, one insists on lighting the torches, would it not be difficult for them to give light? If, when the seasonal rains have come down, one still continues to water the ground, would this not be a waste of labour? Now, you, master, just stand before the throne, and the empire will be in peace; yet I still preside over it. I am conscious of my deficiency, and beg to give to you the empire."

"You, sir, govern the empire," said Hsu Yu, "and it is already in peace. Suppose I were to take your place, would I do it for the name? Name is but the shadow of real gain. [3] Would I do it for real gain? The tit, building its nest in the mighty forest, occupies but a single twig. The tapir, slaking its thirst from the river, drinks only enough to fill its belly. You return and be quiet. I have no need of the empire. Though the cook were not attending to his kitchen, the boy impersonating the dead, and

---

1 One of the traditional sage-kings.
2 A legendary hermit.
3 Reading 賓 as 實, according to Yu Yueh.

the officer of prayer would not step over the cups and stands to take his place."

"The cook, the boy impersonating the dead, and the officer of prayer — all are content with their duties. Birds, beasts, and all things — all are satisfied with their nature. Yao and Hsu Yu, both are quiet in their own positions. In the world, that is the most real gain. Since every one has his real gain, what is the need of artificial activity? All simply enjoy themselves. Therefore, though the conduct of Yao and Hsu Yu was different, their happiness was the same." — *Kuo Hsiang*.

Chien Wu said to Lien Shu: "I heard from Chieh Yu (接輿) some utterances that were great but could not be justified. Once stated, there is no end of his tale. I was greatly startled at what he said. It seemed to be as boundless as the Milky Way. It was very improbable and far removed from human experience."

"What did he say?" asked Lien Shu.

"He said," replied Chien Wu, "far away on the mountain of Ku Yi, there lived a spiritual man. His flesh and skin were like ice and snow. His manner was elegant and graceful as that of a maiden. He did not eat any of the five grains, but inhaled the wind and drank the dew.

The spiritual man transcends all that is material. — *Tr.*

"'He rode on clouds, drove along the flying dragons, and thus rambled beyond the four seas.

He transcends the finite sphere. — *Tr.*

"'His spirit is compact.

His spirit or mind is quiet, calm, and cannot be affected by external things. — *Tr.*

"'Yet he could save things from corruption and secure every year a plentiful harvest.' I thought all these sayings were nonsense and refused to believe in them."

"Yes," said Lien Shu, "the blind have nothing to do with beauty, nor the deaf with music. There are not only physical blindness and deafness, there are also the intellectual. Of the latter you yourself supply an illustration. That man, with those virtues, would embrace all things. According to him, everything in the world is longing for peace; why should there be some who address themselves laboriously to govern the empire?

> Since all things are longing for peace, why not let them alone and get it? — *Tr.*

"That man, nothing can hurt. In a flood reaching the sky, he would not be drowned. In a drought, though metals ran liquid and mountains were scorched, he would not feel hot.

> "There is no lot which the perfect man would not be content with. He is satisfied everywhere. Life and death would not affect him, much less would flood and heat. The perfect man would not be troubled by disasters, not because he can avoid them. According to reason, he goes straightforward, and naturally he meets with the good." — *Kuo Hsiang.*

> Though the perfect man may be harmed, yet his mind is not affected. He cannot be harmed so far as his mind is concerned. — *Tr.*

"Even his dust and siftings could still fashion and mold Yao and Shun.[1] How should he will to occupy himself with things?"

A man of the Sung state carried some ceremonial caps to the Yueh state. But the men of Yueh used to cut off their hair and paint their body, so that they had no use of such things. Yao ruled the people of the empire, and maintained a perfect government within the four seas. He went to see the four sages in the distant mountain of Ku Yi. On returning to his capital south of the Fen River, he silently forgot his empire.

---

1 Another legendary sage-king.

"Yao had no need of the empire, just as the man of Yueh had no need for ceremonial caps. Yet he who has no need of the empire is just the man whom the empire needs for its ruler. Though the empire took Yao as its ruler, Yao himself did not consider the empire as his. He therefore silently forgot it, and let his mind wander in the realm of nondistinction. Though he sat on the throne and controlled all things, there was nothing which could disturb his happiness." — *Kuo Hsiang.*

Hui Tzu[1] said to Chuang Tzu: "The king of Wei sent me some calabash seeds. I planted them and they bore a fruit as big as a five-bushel measure. I used it as a vessel for holding water, but it was not solid enough to hold it. I cut the calabash in two for ladles, but each of them was too shallow to hold anything. Because of this uselessness, I knocked them to pieces."

"Sir," said Chuang Tzu, "it was rather you who did not know how to use large things. There was a man of Sung who had a recipe for salve for chapped hands. From generation to generation, his family made silk washing their occupation. A stranger heard of this and proposed to offer him one hundred ounces of gold for the recipe. The kindred all came together to consider this proposal. 'We have,' said they, 'been washing silk for generations. What we gained is not more than a few ounces of gold. Now in one morning we can sell this art for one hundred ounces. Let us give it to the stranger.' So the stranger got it. He went and informed the king of Wu. When Wu and Yueh were at war, the king of Wu gave him the command of his fleet. In the winter he had a naval engagement with Yueh, in which the latter was totally defeated.

Because the latter had no means to cure chapped hands. — *Tr.*

"The stranger was rewarded with a fief and a title. Thus while the efficiency of the salve to cure the chapped hands was in both cases the same, yet here it secured him a title, there, nothing more

---

1 A prominent scholar of the School of Logicians.

than a capacity for washing silk. This was because its application was different. Now you, sir, have this five-bushel calabash; why did you not make of it a large bottle gourd, by means of which you could float in rivers and lakes? Instead of this, you were sorry that it was useless for holding anything. I think your mind is rather wooly."

Hui Tzu said to Chuang Tzu: "I have a large tree, which men call the ailanthus. Its trunk is so irregular and knotty that a carpenter cannot apply his line to it. Its small branches are so twisted that the square and compasses cannot be used on them. It stands by the roadside, but is not looked at by any carpenter. Now your words, sir, are big but useless and also not wanted by anybody."

Chuang Tzu said: "Have you not seen a wild cat or a weasel? It lies, crouching down, in wait for its prey. East and west it leaps about, avoiding neither what is high nor what is low. At last it is caught in a trap or dies in a net. Again there is the yak, which is as large as the clouds across the sky. But it cannot catch mice. Now you have a large tree and are anxious about its uselessness. Why do you not plant it in the domain of non-existence, in a wide and barren wild? By its side you may wander in nonaction; under it you may sleep in happiness. Neither bill nor ax would shorten its term of existence. Being of no use to others, it itself would be free from harm."

These stories are to show that everything has its particular fitness. Everything is useful in a certain way and useless in another. —Tr.

CHAPTER II
ON THE EQUALITY OF THINGS

"Everything considers itself to be right and others to be wrong, itself to be beautiful and others to be ugly. Everything is what it is. The opinions of the one and the other are different; that they both have opinions is the same." — *Kuo Hsiang.*

Nan Kuo Tzu Chi sat leaning on a table. He looked to heaven and breathed gently, seeming to be in a trance, and unconscious of his body.

Yen Cheng Tzu Yu, who was in attendance on him, said: "What is this? Can the body become thus like dry wood, and the mind like dead ashes? The man leaning on the table is not he who was here before."

"Yen," said Tzu Chi, "your question is very good. Just now, I lost myself, do you understand? You may have heard the music of man, but not the music of earth; you may have heard the music of earth, but not the music of heaven."

"I venture," said Tzu Yu, "to ask from you a general description of these."

"The breath of the universe," said Tzu Chi, "is called the wind. At times, it is inactive. When it is active, angry sounds come from every aperture. Have you not heard the growing roar? The imposing appearance of mountain forest, the apertures and cavities in huge trees many a span in girth: these are like nostrils, like mouth, like ears, like beam sockets, like goblets, like mortars, like pools, like puddles. The wind goes rushing into them, making the sounds of rushing water, of whizzing arrows, of scolding, of breathing, of shouting, of crying, of deep wailing, of moaning agony. Some sounds are shrill, some deep. Gentle winds produce minor harmonies; violent winds, major ones. When the fierce gusts pass away, all the apertures are empty and still. Have you not seen the bending and quivering of the branches and leaves?"

"Not only are the sounds different, but also the movements. The movements may vary in different ways, but they are movements all the same. There is no reason for regarding the bending as especially right, or the quivering as especially wrong." — *Kuo Hsiang.*

"The music of earth," Tzu Yu said, "consists of sounds produced on the various apertures; the music of man, of sounds produced on pipes and flutes. I venture to ask of what consists the music of heaven."

"The winds as they blow," said Tzu Chi, "differ in thousands of ways, yet all are self-produced. Why should there be any other agency to excite them?"

"This is the music of heaven. The music of heaven is not something besides the other two. The different apertures, the pipes and flutes, and other living beings, all together constitutes nature.[1] Since nonbeing is nonbeing, it cannot produce being. When being is not yet produced, it cannot produce other things. Who, then, produces things? They spontaneously produce themselves.... That everything spontaneously becomes what it is, is called natural. Everything is as it is by nature, not made to be so. Therefore, when Chuang Tzu spoke of heaven (*tien*), he meant the natural, not the blue sky.... *Tien* is the general name of all things. There is nothing that can be specifically called *tien*. Who can be the Lord that commands things? Everything produces itself and is not created by others. This is the way of nature." — *Kuo Hsiang.*

There is variety in the blowings of wind. But all of them are equally natural, equally good. So the different things and opinions mentioned in what follows are also equally natural, equally good. — *Tr.*

Great knowledge is wide and comprehensive; small knowledge is partial and restricted. Great speech is rich and powerful; small speech is merely so much talk. When people sleep, there is confusion of soul; When awake, there is movement of body.

---

1 Heaven and nature are both called *tien* in Chinese.

Dream is the "confusion of soul." — *Tr.*

In the association of men with men, there are plotting and scheming; and daily there is striving of mind with mind. There are indecisions, concealments, and reservations. Small apprehensions cause restless distress, great apprehensions cause endless fear. The mind of some flies forth, like a javelin, the arbiter of right and wrong. The mind of others remains firm, like a solemn covenanter, the guardian of rights secured. The mind of some fails like decay in autumn and winter. The mind of others is sunk in sensuous pleasure and cannot come back. The mind of yet others has fixed habits like an old drain; it is near to death and cannot be restored to vigour. Joy and anger, sorrow and pleasure, anxiety and regret, fickleness and determination, vehemence and indolence, indulgence and extravagance: these come like music sounding from an empty tube, or mushrooms springing out of warmth and moisture. Daily and nightly they alternate within us, but we cannot tell whence they spring. Can we expect in a moment to find out how they are produced?

The above is a description of the variety of psychological conditions. They are spontaneously produced just as "music sounding from an empty tube, or mushrooms springing out of warmth and moisture." They are produced by no Creator, just as the music of earth needs no special agency to excite it. — *Tr.*

If there is no other, there will be no I. If there is no I, there will be none to make distinctions. This seems to be true. But what causes these varieties? It might seem as if there would be a real Lord, but there is no indication of His existence. One may believe that He exists, but we do not see His form. He may have reality, but no form. The hundred parts of the human body, with its nine openings, and six viscera, all are complete in their places. Which shall I prefer? Do you like them all equally? Or do you like some more than others? Are they all servants? Are these servants unable to control each other, but need another as ruler? Do they become rulers and servants in turn? Is there any true ruler other than themselves? Regarding these questions, whether we can obtain true answers or not, it matters but little to the reality of the ruler (if there is one).

> In the macrocosm, there is no real Lord other than the variety of things. There is no God. In the microcosm there is no real ruler other than the different parts of the body. There is no soul. — *Tr.*

When once we have received the bodily form complete, its parts do not fail to perform their functions till the end comes. In conflict with things or in harmony with them, they pursue their course with the speed of a galloping horse which cannot be stopped; is it not deplorable? To be constantly toiling all the time of one's life, without seeing the fruit of one's labour; to be weary and worn out, without knowing where one is going to; is it not lamentable? Man may say: there is immortality. But what is the use of this saying? When the body is decomposed, so with it is the spirit. Can it not be called very deplorable? Is the life of man, indeed, so ignorant? Am I the only one who is ignorant, but are there others who are not?

> This is a general description of life. Kuo Hsiang said: "Compared with what people usually consider as deplorable, life is cretainly deplorable. The fact that people usually do not consider life as deplorable shows that there is nothing deplorable. All things are what they are, without knowing why and how they are. Therefore all things are ignorant. Those who know do know, without knowing why and how they know. Those who live do live, without knowing why and how they live. Although things are different, yet they are the same in that they live without knowing why and how they live. Therefore all things in the world are ignorant."

If men are to be guided by opinions, who will not have such a guide? Not only those who know the alternations of right and wrong and choose between them have opinions; the fools have theirs too. The case in which there are no opinions, while yet a distinction is made between right and wrong, is as inconceivable as that one goes to Yueh to-day, but arrived there yesterday. That is to make what is not is. How to make what is not is, even holy Yu[1] could not know. How can I do it?

> This shows that all distinctions of right and wrong are due to opinions. — *Tr.*

Speech is not merely the blowing of winds. It is intending to say something. But what it is intending to say is not absolutely established.

> What is affirmed by one may be denied by another. — *Tr.*

Is there really such a thing as speech? Is there really no such thing as speech? Someone considers speech as different from the chirping of young birds. But is there any distinction between them, or is there no distinction?

How is *Tao* obscured that there should be a distinction between true and false? How is speech obscured that there should be a distinction between right and wrong? Where is *Tao* not present? Where is speech not appropriate?

> *Tao* is everywhere present; speech is everywhere appropriate. In Chuang Tzu's book, Chapter XVII, "Autumn Floods," Chuang Tzu said: "From the point of view of *Tao*, in things there is no distinction of value and worthlessness. From the point of view of things, everything values itself and considers others worthless. . . . If we say a thing is great, because it is considered great by something, then everything is great. If we say a thing is small, because it is considered small by something, then everything is small. . . . If we say a thing is right, because it is considered right by something, then everything is right. If we say a thing is wrong, because it is considered wrong by something, then everything is wrong." Any word can be the predicate of anything. Every word is appropriate everywhere. — *Tr.*

Tao is obscured by partiality. Speech is obscured by eloquence. The result is the affirmations and denials of the Confucianists and Mohists; the one regarding as right what the other regards

---

1 A legendary sage-king.

as wrong, and regarding as wrong what the other regards as right. If we are to affirm what these two schools both deny, and to deny what they both affirm, there is nothing better than to use the light of reason.

"That there is a distinction of right and wrong is what the Confucianists and the Mohists affirm. That there is no such distinction is what they deny. To affirm what they deny and to deny what they affirm is to show there is no such distinction." — *Kuo Hsiang.*

Everything is "that" (another thing's other); everything is "this" (its own self). Things do not know that they are another's "that"; they only know that they are "this." The "that" and the "this" produce each other. Nevertheless, when there is life, there is death, and when there is death, there is life. When there is possibility, there is impossibility, and when there is impossibility, there is possibility. Because there is right, there is wrong. Because there is wrong, there is right. On account of this fact, the sages do not take this way, but see things in the light of Heaven. The "this" is also "that." The "that" is also "this." The "that" has a system of right and wrong. The "this" also has a system of right and wrong. Is there really a distinction between "that" and "this"? Or is there really no distinction between "that" and "this"? That the "that" and the "this" cease to be opposites is the very essence of *Tao*. Only the essence, an axis as it were, is the centre of the circle responding to the endless changes. The right is an endless change. The wrong is also an endless change. Therefore it is said that there is nothing better than to use the light of reason.

All distinctions of right and wrong are due to opinion. That which can reveal the falsity of opinion is reason. Reason "sees things in the light of Heaven," and knows that the "systems of right and wrong" are human judgments and have nothing to do with nature. To see this is "the very essence of *Tao*." — *Tr.*

To take fingers in illustration of fingers as not being fingers, is not so good as to take non-fingers in illustration of fingers as not being fingers. To take a white horse in illustration of horses as not being horses, is not so good as to take non-horses in illustration of horses as not being horses. The universe is a finger; all things are a horse.

> "In order to show that there is no distinction between right and wrong, there is nothing better than illustrating one thing by another. In illustrating one thing by another, we see that all things agree in that they all consider themselves to be right and others to be wrong. Since they all agree that all others are wrong, so in the world there can be no right. Since they all agree that they themselves are all right, so in the world there can be no wrong. How can it be shown that this is so? If the right is really absolutely right, there should be none that considers it to be wrong. If the wrong is really absolutely wrong, there should be none that considers it to be right. The fact that there are uncertainly between right and wrong and the confusions in distinctions shows that the distinction of right and wrong is due to partiality of view, and that things are really in agreement. In our observation, we see this truth everywhere. Therefore, the perfect man, knowing that the universe is a finger and all things are a horse, thus rests in great peace. All things function according to their nature. They all enjoy themselves. There is no distinction between right and wrong."
> — *Kuo Hsiang.*

> This is an illustration of the theory that to attack one system of right and wrong with another is not so good as to attack the whole system of rights and wrongs with the system of nondistinction between right and wrong. The argument about the finger and the horse was one used by the School of Logicians. The logicians said there is an absolute distinction between right and wrong; the Taoists said there is no such absolute distinction. The one school emphasized the distinctions or the differences between things; the other school stressed nondistinction or the sameness. Hence the two schools were always in dispute with each other. — *Tr.*

The possible is possible. The impossible is impossible. The *Tao* makes things and they are what they are. What are they? They are what they are. What are they not? They are not what they are not. Everything is something and is good for something. There is nothing which is not something or is not

45

good for something. Thus it is that there are roof-slats and pillars, ugliness and beauty, the peculiar and the extraordinary. All these by means of the *Tao* are united and become one. To make a distinction is to make some construction. But construction is the same as destruction. For things as a whole there is neither construction nor destruction, but they turn to unity and become one. Only the truly intelligent knows the unity of things. They therefore do not make distinctions, but follow the common and the ordinary. The common and the ordinary are the natural functions of all things, which express the common nature of the whole. Following the common nature of the whole, they are happy. Being happy, they are near perfection. Perfection is for them to stop. They stop, yet they do not know that they stop. This is *Tao*.

To wear out one's spirit and intelligence in order to unify things without knowing that they are already in agreement, is called "three in the morning." What is "three in the morning"? A keeper of monkeys once ordered concerning the monkey's rations of acorns that each monkey was to have three in the morning and four at night. But at this the monkeys were very angry. So the keeper said that they might have four in the morning, but three at night. With this arrangement, all monkeys were well pleased. The actual number of acorns remained the same, but there was a difference as to the monkey's feeling of pleasure and anger. So the keeper acted accordingly. Therefore, the sages harmonize the systems of right and wrong, and rest in the evolution of nature. This is called following two courses at once.

Although the systems of right and wrong are but human judgments and have no validity from the "point of view of nature," yet that people do pass these invalid judgments is a fact. This fact is a natural phenomenon just as anything else. So the sages "rest in the evolution of nature," just let the different opinions alone, and do not dispute or interfere with them. They do not abolish the different opinions; they just transcend them. This is called following two courses at once. — *Tr.*

The knowledge of the ancients was perfect. How perfect?

At first, they did not yet know that there were things. This is the most perfect knowledge; nothing can be added. Next, they knew that there were things, but did not yet make distinctions between them. Next they made distinctions between them, but they did not yet pass judgments upon them. When judgments were passed, *Tao* was destroyed. With the destruction of *Tao*, individual preferences came into being. Are there really construction and destruction? Is there really no construction and no destruction? That there are construction and destruction is like the fact that Chao Wen played the lute. That there is no construction and no destruction is like the fact that Chao Wen did not play the lute.

> "All tunes cannot be played at once. When playing a piece of music, no matter how many hands take part in it, there must be some tunes left unplayed. To play music is to make the tunes known. But by making it known one gets only a part; by not making it known, one gets the whole. Therefore, the fact that Chao Wen played the lute was to destroy something by constructing something. The fact that Chao Wen did not play the lute was to destroy nothing by constructing nothing." — *Kuo Hsiang.*

Chao Wen played the lute. Shih Kuang wielded the stick to keep time. Hui Tzu argued, leaning against a dryandra tree. The knowledge of each of the three masters in their arts was nearly perfect, and therefore each practised it to the end of his life. Because they were fond of it, they wished to enlighten people in it. But people were not to be enlightened by their art. So Hui Tzu ended with the obscure discussion of hardness and whiteness.

> Another argument used by the School of Logicians. — *Tr.*

Chao Wen's son continued to play on his father's string, and ended with no accomplishment. If this can be called accomplishment, even I accomplish something. If this cannot be called accomplishment, neither I nor others accomplish anything. Therefore what the sages aim at is the light out of darkness. Therefore, they do not make distinctions and stop at the ordinary. This is called using the light of reason.

In these paragraphs, Chuang Tzu gradually passed from the discussion of the rational knowledge of the nondistinction of right and wrong to that of the mystic experience of the union of the individual with the whole. This union is attained in the world of pure experience, to use James's terminology. The "ancients" simply take pure experience, the immediate presentation, "the *that* in short (for until we have decided *what* it is, it must be a mere *that*)."[1] "They simply take the *that* at its face value, neither more nor less; and taking it at its value means, first of all, to take it just as we feel it, and not to confuse ourselves with abstract talk *about* it, involving words that drive us to invent secondary conceptions in order to mentalize their suggestions and make our actual experience again seem rationally possible."[2] In this state there is an unbroken flux of experience, but the experiencer does not *know* it. The "ancients" did not know that there are things, to say nothing of making distinctions between them. There is no separation between things, to say nothing of the distinction between the subject and the object. So in this state of experience there is nothing but the one. — *Tr.*

"The ancients forget heaven and earth, and neglect all things. Outwardly they have no conscious observation of the world. Inwardly they have no conscious feeling of their own body. Therefore they are free and without trouble. They go with everything and adapt everywhere." — *Kuo Hsiang.*

Now I have something to say. I do not know whether or not what I shall say is of the same character as what others say. In one sense, what I say is not of the same character. In another sense, what I say is of the same character, and there is no differenco between what I say and what others say. But though this may be the case, let me try to explain myself. There is beginning, there is no beginning. There is no no-beginning. There is being, there is nonbeing. There is no nonbeing. There is no no-nonbeing. Suddenly there is a distinction of being and nonbeing. Still, between being and nonbeing, I do not know which is

---

1 William James, *Essays in Radical Empiricism*, p. 13.
2 *Id.*, pp. 48, 49.

48

really being and which is really nonbeing. I have just said something; but I do not know whether what I have said is really something said or not really something said. There is nothing larger in the world than the point of a hair, yet Mount Tai is small. There is nothing older than a dead child, yet Peng Tsu had an untimely death. Heaven and Earth and I came into existence together, and all things with me are one. Since all things are one, what room is there for speech? But since I have already spoken of the one, is this not already speech? One plus speech makes two. Two plus one makes three. Going on from this, even the most skillful reckoner will not be able to reach the end, and how much less able to do so are ordinary people! If proceeding from nothing to something we can reach three, how much further shall we reach, if we proceed from something to something! Let us not proceed. Let us stop here.

In the state of pure experience, we have no intellectual knowledge of any kind. In connection with time, or with things in time, we have no intellectual knowledge of beginning. We have no intellectual knowledge of the fact that we have no intellectual knowledge of beginning. In connection with space, or with things in space, we have no intellectual knowledge of being. We have no intellectual knowledge of the fact that we have no intellectual knowledge of being. We have no intellectual knowledge of the fact that we have no intellectual knowledge of the fact that we have no intellectual knowledge of being. Thus, in the state of pure experience, though ontologically there may be still distinctions and differences, yet epistemologically there are none. Epistemologically the individual is one with the whole. — Tr.

Tao has no distinctions. Speech cannot be applied to the eternal. Because of speech, there are demarcations. Let me say something about the demarcations. There are the right and the left, discussions and judgments, divisions and arguments, emulations and contentions. These are called the eight predicables. What is beyond this world, the sages do not discuss, although they do not deny its existence. What is within this world, the sages discuss, but do not pass judgments. About the chronicle history, and records of ancient kings, the sages pass judgment but do not argue. When there is division, there is something not divided. When there is argument, there is something which the argument does not reach. How is that? The sages embrace all things, while men in general argue about them in order to convince each other. Great *Tao* does not admit of being spoken. Great argument does not require words. Great benevolence is not purposely charitable. Great purity is not purposely modest. Great courage is not purposely violent. *Tao* that is displayed is not *Tao*. Speech that argues falls short of its aim. Benevolence that is constantly exercised does not accomplish its object. Purity, if openly professed, meets incredulity. Courage that is purposely violent must itself fail. These five are, as it were, round, yet tend to become square. Therefore, he who knows to stop at what he does not know, is perfect. He who knows the argument that requires no words and the *Tao* that cannot be named, is called the store of nature. The store, when things are put in it, is not full, when things are taken out, it is not empty; yet he himself does not know why it is so. This is called the preservation of enlightenment.

> This shows the limitation of finite qualities. One should give qualities up, should stop at pure experience, and so be one with the infinite. — *Tr.*

Of old, Yao said to Shun, "I would attack the states of Tsung, Kuei, and Hsu Ao. Ever since I have been on the throne, I have not been able to put them out of my mind. Why is it so?"

"The rulers of these three states," replied Shun, "are still living primitively among the mugwort and the brushwood. Why do you not put them out of your mind? Once upon a time, ten suns came out together, and all things were illuminated thereby. How much more should virtue illuminate, since virtue excels the suns?"

> "Although the sun and the moon have no selfish preference in their illumination, yet there are still things beyond their range. But in virtue there is nothing unhappy. If one attempts to change the aspiration

50

of the people who live in the mugwort and brushwood and to compel them to follow one's self, one is not in agreement with the comprehensiveness of *Tao*. . . . Let everything enjoy its own nature, and have its own satisfaction. No matter whatever and wherever things may be, leave them alone each in its own proper sphere. Then they are content, and we also are happy." — *Kuo Hsiang*.

This shows the equality of civilization and barbarism. There is a variety in the ways of living, just as there is a variety in things. These different ways are of equal value. — *Tr.*

Yeh Chueh asked Wang Yi, saying: "Do you know in what all things agree?"

"How can I know?" answered Wang Yi.

"Do you know what you do not know?" Yeh Chueh again asked.

"How can I know?" Wang Yi answered again.

"Then do all things have no knowledge?" asked Yeh Chueh for the third time.

"How can I know?" answered Wang Yi "Nevertheless, I shall try to say something. How can I know that what I say I know may not be really what I do not know? How can I know that what I say I do not know may be really what I know? Now I would ask you some questions. If a man sleeps in a damp place, he will have a pain in his loins, and half his body will be as if it were dead. But is it so with an eel? If a man lives up in a tree, he will be frightened and all in a tremble. But is it so with a monkey? Among these three, who knows the right way of habitation? Men eat flesh; deer feed on grass. Centipedes enjoy snakes; owls and crows delight in mice. Among these four, who knows the right taste? Monkey mates with monkey; the buck with the doe. Mao Chiang and Li Chi were considered by men as the most beautiful of women; but at the sight of them fish dived deep in the water, birds soared up in the air, and deer hurried away. Among these four, who knows the right standard of beauty? As I look at this matter, the principles of benevolence and righteousness, the ways of right and wrong, are inextricably mixed and confused. How could I know the difference among them?"

"If you," asked Yeh Chueh, "do not know what is beneficial and what is harmful, does not this mean that the perfect man is without this knowledge?"

"The perfect man is mysterious," replied Wang Yi. "Were the great lakes burned up, he would not feel hot. Were the great rivers frozen hard, he would not feel cold. Were the mountains to be riven with thunder, or the seas thrown into waves by a storm, he would not be frightened. Being such, he would mount upon the clouds of heaven, would ride on the sun and moon, and would thus ramble at ease beyond the seas. Neither death nor life can affect him; how much less can the consideration of what is beneficial and what is harmful?"

Chu Chiao Tzu asked Chang Wu Tzu, saying: "I heard from the Master, the sage does not occupy himself with the affairs of the world. He neither seeks gain, nor avoids injury. He has no pleasure in seeking. He does not purposely adhere to *Tao*. He speaks without speaking. He does not speak when he speaks. Thus he roams beyond the limits of this dusty world. The Master considered this as a rough description of the sage, but I consider this as the ways of the mysterious *Tao*. How do you think of it, my dear sir?"

"These points," said Chang Wu Tzu, "would have perplexed even the Yellow Emperor; how could Confucius be competent to understand them? Moreover, you are too hasty in forming your estimate. You see an egg, and immediately you expect to hear it crow. You look at the crossbow, and immediately you expect to have a roast dove before you. I shall speak a few words with you at random, and do you also listen to them at random? How does the sage sit by the sun and the moon, and hold the universe in his arms? He blends everything into a harmonious whole, rejects the confusion of distinctions, and ignores the differences in social rank. Men in general bustle about and toil; the sage is primitive and without knowledge. He blends together ten thousand years, and stops at the one, the whole, and the simple. All things are what they are, and spontaneously pursue their courses. How do I know that the love of life is not a delusion? How do I know that he who is afraid of death is not like a man who was away from his home when young and therefore has no intention to return? Li Chi was the daughter of the border warden of Ai. When the state of Tsin first got her, she wept until the front part of her robe was drenched with tears. But when she came to the royal residence, shared with the king his luxurious couch and ate rich food, she regretted that she had wept. How do I know that the dead will not repent of their former craving for life? Those who dream of a banquet at night may in the next morning wail and weep. Those who dream of wailing and weeping may in the morning go out to hunt. When they dream, they do not know that they are dreaming. In their dream, they may even interpret dreams. Only when they are awake, they begin to know that they dreamed. By and by comes the great awakening, and then we shall find out that life itself is a great dream. All the while, the fools think that they are awake; that they know. With nice discriminations, they make distinctions between princes and grooms. How stupid! Confucius and you are both in a dream. When I say that you are in a dream, I am also in a dream. This saying is called a paradox. If after ten thousand ages, we could once meet a great sage who knows how to explain it, it would be as if we meet him in a very short time.

"Suppose that you argue with me. If you beat me, instead of my beating you, are you necessarily right and am I necessarily wrong? Or, if I beat you, and not you me, am I necessarily right and are you necessarily wrong? Is one of us right and the other wrong? Or are both of us right or both of us wrong? Neither you nor I can know, and others are all the more in the dark. Whom shall we ask to produce the right decision? We may ask someone who agrees with you; but since he agrees with you, how can he make the decision? We may ask someone who agrees with me; but since he agrees with me, how can he make the decision? We may ask someone who agrees with both you and me; but since he agrees with both you and me, how can he make the decision? We may ask someone who differs from both you and me; but since he differs from both you and me, how can he make the decision? In this way, you and I and others all would not be able to come to a mutual and common understanding; shall we wait for still another?"

Whether the changing sounds

The arguments of right and wrong.

are relative to one another or not, we just harmonize them within the boundary of nature, and leave them alone in the process of natural evolution. This is the way to complete our lifetime. What is meant by harmonizing things within the boundary of nature? Referring to the right and the wrong, the "being so" and the "not being so": if the right is really right, we need not dispute about how it is different from the wrong; if the "being so" is really being so, we need not dispute about how it is different from "not being so".... Let us forget life. Let us forget the distinction between right and wrong. Let us take our joy in the realm of the infinite and remain there. [1]

The Penumbra asked the Shadow, saying, "At one moment, you move; at another, you are at rest. At one moment, you sit down; at another, you stand up. Why this instability of purpose?"

"Do I have to depend upon something else," replied the Shadow, "in order to be what I am? Does that something upon which I depend still have to depend upon something else in order to be what it is? Do I have to depend upon the scales of a snake or the wings of a cicada? How can I tell why I am so, or why I am not otherwise?"

This shows that everything is spontaneously what it is. One needs only to follow one's nature and not to ask why one is so and not otherwise. — Tr.

Once upon a time, Chuang Chou [2] dreamed that he was a butterfly, a butterfly flying about, enjoying itself. It did not know

---

1 This paragraph is rearranged according to Wang Hsien-chien.
2 Chou was Chuang Tzu's name.

that it was Chuang Chou. Suddenly he awoke, and veritably was Chuang Chou again. We do not know whether it was Chuang Chou dreaming that he was a butterfly, or whether it was the butterfly dreaming that it was Chuang Chou. Between Chuang Chou and the butterfly there must be some distinction. This is a case of what is called the transformation of things.

This shows that, although in ordinary appearance there are differences between things, in delusions or in dreams one thing can also be another. "The transformation of things" proves that the differences among things are not absolute. — *Tr.*

CHAPTER III
THE FUNDAMENTALS FOR
THE CULTIVATION OF LIFE

There is a limit to our life, but to knowledge there is no limit. With what is limited to pursue what is unlimited is a perilous thing. When knowing this, we still seek to increase our knowledge, the peril cannot be averted. In doing what convention considers as good, eschew fame. In doing what convention considers as bad, escape disgrace or penalty. Always pursue the middle course. These are the ways to preserve our body, to maintain our life, to support our parents, to complete our terms of years.

Prince Wen Hui's cook was cutting up a bullock. Every blow of his hand, every heave of his shoulder, every tread of his foot, every thrust of his knee, every sound of the rending flesh, and every note of the movement of the chopper were in perfect harmony — rhythmical like the dance of "The Mulberry Grove,"[1] simultaneous like the chords of the "Ching Shou."[1]

"Ah, admirable," said the prince, "that your art should become so perfect!"

The cook laid down his chopper and replied: "What your servant loves is *Tao*, which is more advanced than art. When I first began to cut up bullocks, what I saw was simply whole bullocks. After three years' practice, I saw no more bullocks as wholes. At present, I work with my mind, but not with my eyes. The functions of my senses stop; my spirit dominates. Following the natural veins,[2] my chopper slips through the great cavities, slides through the great openings, taking advantage of what is already there. I did not attempt the central veins and their branches, and the connectives between flesh and bone, not to mention the great bones. A good cook changes his chopper once a year, because he cuts. An ordinary cook changes his chopper once a

---

1 Two pieces of music.

2 Here the word 理 is used in its original meaning; viz., the lines or the veins in the jade.

month, because he hacks. Now my chopper has been in use for nineteen years; it has cut up several thousand bullocks; yet its edge is as sharp as if it just came from the whetstone. At the joints there are always interstices, and the edge of the chopper is without .thickness. If we insert that which is without thickness into an interstice, there is certainly plenty of room for it to move along. Nevertheless, when I come to a complicated joint, and see that there will be some difficulty, I proceed anxiously and with caution. I fix my eyes on it. I move slowly. Then by a very gentle movement of my chopper, the part is quickly separated, and yields like earth crumbling to the ground. Then standing with the chopper in my hand, I look all round, with an air of triumph and satisfaction. Then I wipe my chopper and put it in its sheath."

"Excellent," said the prince, "from the words of this cook, I learned the ways of cultivating life."

This story shows that in life, there are always natural ways of doing things, natural solutions of problems. If we can do things according to the natural way, things will be done without any trouble to our mind. Our mind will be always fresh as the chopper of the cook. — Tr.

When Kung Wen Hsien saw the Master of the Right, he was startled, and said: "Who is he? How is it that he has but one foot? Is this due to nature or due to man?"

"This is due to nature, not to man," said the Master of the Right. "Nature produces the foot and causes it to be this one only. The appearances of man are well balanced. From this I know it is due to nature, not to man."

"That which is well balanced is due to nature, so to have only one foot is not particularly due to the fault of the individual. Therefore, those who know the reality of life would do nothing regarding what cannot be helped. Those who know the essentials of destiny would simply follow its appointment. They simply maintain what is natural." — Kuo Hsiang.

The pheasant of the marshes gets a peck once in ten steps,

a drink once in a hundred. Yet it does not want to be fed in a cage. In the marshes, its spirit is healthy, and consequently it forgets health.

These show that those who cultivate life best are those who culti-vate their spirit best. To cultivate the spirit best is to set it free. If the spirit is in good condition, so also is the life, even though the body be in bad condition, as was the case with the Master of the Right. If the spirit is in bad condition, so also is the life, even though the body is in good condition, as was the case with the pheasant in a cage. Free-dom of the spirit is essential to the cultivation of life. — *Tr.*

When Lao Tzu died, Chin Shih went to mourn over him. He uttered three yells and went out.

A disciple asked him, saying, "Were you not a friend of the master?"

"Yes, I was," replied Chin Shih.

"If so, is it proper to offer your mourning merely in the way you have done?"

"Yes," said Chin Shih. "At first, I thought the other mourn-ers were his [Lao Tzu's] men; now I know they are not. When I went in to mourn, there were old persons weeping as if for the loss of their children; and young ones, as if for that of their mother. These persons assembled there, uttered words, and dropped tears, which are not to be expected. This is to violate the princi-ple of nature and to increase the emotion of man, forgetting what we have received from nature. These were called by the ancients the penalty of violating the principle of nature. When the Master came, it was because he had the occasion to be born. When he went, he simply followed the natural course. Those who are quiet at the proper occasion and follow the natural course cannot be affected by sorrow or joy. They were considered by the an-cients as the men of the gods, who were released from bondage.

"Of what we have received from nature, there is a proper amount, which can neither be increased nor decreased with human effort. He who has too much affection and attempts what is beyond the most proper, thus violates the principle of nature. He will bustle in the

61

sphere of sorrow and joy. He thus suffers, though no actual punishment may be inflicted upon him. Is not this a kind of penalty? Sorrow and joy are the results of loss and gain. The profound and intelligent man, identifying himself with change itself, would be quiet at any occasion and follow any course. He is one with evolution; he is everywhere. To him there is neither gain nor loss, neither death nor life. He would take whatever he meets and thus experience neither sorrow nor joy. Whenever there is attachment, there is bondage. If there is no attachment, the bondage is released. When the bondage is released, there is happiness. This is the essence of cultivating life." — *Kuo Hsiang*.

The punishment of violating the principle of nature is what Spinoza called human bondage, which is caused by the increase of human emotions. To know the limitation of the nature of man is to attain what Spinoza called human freedom, the "release from bondage." When one can conceive things under the form of eternity, to use Spinoza's phraseology, one would not be affected by emotions. — *Tr*.

"The fingers may not be able to supply all the fuel. But the fire is transmitted, and we know not when it will come to an end."

This is Chuang Tzu's conception of immortality. His conception does not presuppose a spiritualistic universe, a universe whose science and naturalistic philosophy cannot admit. The body of the individual must die, so does his soul, which is the function of the body. But the universe as a whole must eternally exist; so do those also who identify themselves with the whole. Chiao Hung, one of the commentators of Chuang Tzu in the Ming Dynasty, said: "Though the waves may cease to exist, the sea is still there. The sea has neither life nor death. In other parts of this chapter, Chuang Tzu spoke of cultivating life. In this part he said that life and death are one. There is no contradiction. He who knows that life and death are one is he who cultivates life best. —*Tr*.

CHAPTER IV
THE HUMAN WORLD

"Since we are living with men, we cannot get away from them. But the human world is always changing; one generation is different from another. Only those who have no prejudice and do not insist on their own selves can follow the changes and not suffer." — *Kuo Hsiang.*

Yen Hui[1] went to see Confucius and asked leave to take his departure. "Where are you going?" asked the Master.

"I am going to the state of Wei" (衛), was the reply.

"With what object?"

"I hear the prince of Wei is in the vigour of his youth, and is determined in his action. He behaves as if the state were of no importance, and will not see his own faults. He thinks lightly of his people's death, and consequently the dead are lying all over the country like so much undergrowth in the marsh. The people know not where to turn. Once you, Master, told me: 'Leave the state that is well governed; go to the state where disorder prevails.' At the door of a physician there are many who are ill. Through what I heard from you, I wish to think out some method, with which perchance I may cure the evils of Wei."

"Alas!" said Confucius, "I am afraid you will only succeed in giving suffering and punishment to yourself. The right method does not admit of any admixture. When there is admixture, the one method will become many. When there are many methods, there is confusion. When there is confusion, there is embarrassment. When there is embarrassment, the situation cannot be saved. The perfect man of the ancients was required to take care of himself before taking care of others. If in taking care of one's self, there is still something unestablished, what leisure has one to attend to the conduct of the wicked man? Besides, do you know where virtue is spoiled, where knowledge begins? Virtue is spoiled with desire for fame; knowledge begins when there is

---

1 A disciple of Confucius.

contention. Contending for fame, men crush each other; and knowledge is the weapon for contention. Both are instruments of evil and should have no place in one's conduct. There are some men who have solid virtue, firm sincerity, and a disposition to disregard renown and fame, but no knowledge of the nature and the mind of man. Notwithstanding, they forcibly impose the teaching of benevolence, righteousness, and rules upon the wicked. Consequently, they are hated for the very reason that they are good. This is called to hurt others. Those who hurt others must be hurt by them in return. Such probably will be your end!

"Besides, if the prince likes the good and hates the bad, what object will you have in inviting him to change his ways? If he does not so, you can only be silent. If you are not so and begin to announce your views, the prince will take the opportunity to contend with you for victory. Your eyes will be dazzled and full of perplexity. Your expression will fade. Your mouth will frame words to excuse yourself. Your manner will express your inner confusion. Your mind will tend to confirm what he said. This will be to quell fire with fire, water with water, increasing, as we may say, the evils. If you begin with concessions, there will be no end of it. If you insist on your own good words which he does not believe, you will die in the hand of the tyrant. Formerly, Chieh[1] killed Kuan Lung Pang[2]; and Chou,[1] Prince Pi Kan[2]. These two victims were both men who cultivated virtue themselves in order to secure the welfare of others' people. In a position of inferior, they thus offended their superiors. Therefore, because of their very moral virtue, their rulers crushed them. All struggled for fame. Of old, Yao attacked the states of Tsung Chi （叢技） and Hsu Ao; Yu attacked the state of Yu Hu. These states were destroyed and the rulers were killed. They had engaged in war without ceasing; their craving for real gain was insatiable. These persons were either for fame or real gain; have you not heard of them? Even the sages failed in their effort to overcome the desire for fame and real gain; can you suc-

---

1 Two tyrants of antiquity.
2 Their worthy ministers.

66

ceed? Nevertheless, you must have a plan of your own; try to tell me what it is."

"Gravity of demeanour and dispassionateness, energy and singleness of purpose," said Yen Hui, "will these do?"

"No," said Confucius, "those will not do! The prince of Wei is full of a masterful spirit and makes much show of himself. His mood is uncertain. Ordinarily he is opposed by nobody. So he has come to take actual pleasure in trampling upon the feeling of others. If he has thus failed in the practice of routine virtues, do you expect that he will be ready to take the higher ones? He will be obstinate and refuse to be converted. He may outwardly agree with you, but inwardly there will be no self-condemnation. How can you succeed?"

"Well, then," said Yen Hui, "while inwardly maintaining my uprightness, I will outwardly seem to be crooked. I will substantiate what I say by appealing to antiquity. Inwardly maintaining my uprightness, I shall be a follower of nature. He who is a follower of nature knows that the prince and he himself are equally the children of nature. Will he care whether what he said will be approved or disapproved? Such a man will be considered by others as a child. This is what I call being a follower of nature. Outwardly seeming to be crooked, I shall be a follower of men. Bowing, kneeling, bending the body, these are the observances of the ministers. What all men do, none will blame me for doing. This is what I call being a follower of men. Substantiating what I said by appealing to antiquity, I shall be a follower of the ancients. Although the words I say are really instructive and condemnatory, yet they are those of the ancients, not my own. In this way, though upright, I shall be free from blame. This is what I call being a follower of the ancients. Will these do?"

"No," said Confucius, "that will not do. You have too many plans; they are right but not skillful. Though rigid, they save you from harm. But that is all; they are not the most perfect. You still made your prejudice your guide."

"I can go no further," said Yen Hui. "I venture to ask you for a method."

"Fast," replied Confucius. "Then I shall tell you. If you

have preju dice, do you think it will be easy to deal with things? He who thinks it will be easy will meet the disapproval of bright heaven."

"My family is poor," said Yen Hui, "and for many months I have tasted neither wine nor meat. Can this be regarded as fasting?"

"This is the fasting appropriate to sacrificing," replied Confucius, "but not the fasting of mind."

"I venture to ask what fasting of mind is," said Yen Hui.

"Maintain the unity of your will," said Confucius. "Do not listen with ears, but with the mind. Do not listen with the mind, but with the spirit. The function of the ear ends with hearing;[1] that of the mind, with symbols or ideas. But the spirit is an emptiness ready to receive all things. *Tao* abides in the emptiness; the emptiness is the fast of mind."

"When I do not try the fasting of mind," said Yen Hui, "I retain my individuality. When I try it, I no longer have my individuality. Can this be called empty?"

"Exactly," replied Confucius. "Let me tell you. Enter this man's service, but do not contend for fame. If he finds you agreeable, you may make some noise; if not, you keep silent.

"Speech must be made as musical notes which respond without any effort of conscious mind. To speak is just to make some noise. To respond without conscious mind is to let things alone and to force nothing upon them." — *Kuo Hsiang.*

"Do not show any conspicuous method; do not exhibit any conspicuous object.[2] Live at the one and stop with what you cannot help.

"What one cannot help is what is necessary in reason." — *Kuo Hsiang.*

"Then you will be nearly successful. It is easy to stop walking, but rather difficult to walk without touching the ground.

1 Reading 聴止於耳 as 耳止於聴, according to Yu Yueh.
2 Reading 毒 as 壔, according to Li Chen.

"It is easy to do nothing, but rather difficult to do something without hurting the spirit." — *Kuo Hsiang.*

"Acting in the manner of man, it is easy to be artificial. Acting in the manner of nature, it is difficult to be artificial. I have heard of flying with wings, but not of flying without them. I have heard of knowing with knowledge, but not of knowing without it. Look at that which is empty. In the empty room, there is bright light, there is happiness. If you cannot stop there, your mind is galloping abroad though your body is sitting. If you can keep your ears and eyes to communicate within, and shut out consciousness and knowledge, then even the supernatural will live with you, not to mention man. This is the mystery of things. This was the hinge on which Yu and Shun moved. This was what Fu Hsi and Chi Chu practised through their lives. How much more would others follow the same rule."

> This story shows that emptiness, to be without individuality, without self, is the best way to deal with man, the best way to live in the world of men. To be without self is the essence of Chuang Tzu's doctrine. "The perfect man has no self," as he said in the first chapter. If one can really be without self in the human world, he will offend no one. "An avenger does not snap in twain the murderous weapon; neither does the most spiteful man carry his resentment to a tile which may have hit him on the head." (See Chapter XIX, Giles's translation, p. 232.) — *Tr.*

Tzu Kao, duke of She, being about to go on a mission to the state of Chi, asked Confucius, saying: "The king is sending me on a mission which is very important. The state of Chi will probably receive me as an ambassador with great respect, but will not be in a hurry to attend to the business. Even an ordinary man cannot be easily pushed, still less a prince of a state. I am full of apprehension. You always told me that in all undertaking, great or small, *Tao* alone leads to a happy issue. In my case, if I cannot succeed, there will be trouble from men.

Punishments from the king. — *Tr.*

69

"If I could succeed, there will be trouble from nature.

The suffering of anxiety and overjoy. — *Tr.*

"Only the man of virtue can be free from these troubles, whether he succeeds or fails. I am not dainty with food. In the kitchen there is no man who needs cooling drinks.

The kitchen is very simple. — *Tr.*

"Yet in the morning I received my charge, and in the evening I have been drinking iced water. I am hot inside. Even before engaging in the actual business, I am already suffering trouble from nature. If I cannot succeed, I certainly will suffer trouble from men. That means I will suffer both troubles, which are more than I, as a minister, can bear. Can you tell me what is to be done?"

"In the world," said Confucius, "there are two great binding principles. The one is destiny; the other is duty. A child's love for its parents is destiny; it is inseparable from the child's heart. A subject's allegiance to his sovereign is duty; he must have a sovereign; there is no escape in the world. These are the two great binding principles. Therefore, to serve one's parents willingly, no matter what condition one is in, is the perfection of filial piety. To serve one's sovereign willingly, no matter what he asks to have done, is the height of loyalty. To serve one's own spirit so as to permit neither joy nor sorrow within, but to consider the inevitable as the appointment of destiny and to be at ease there, is the perfection of virtue. He who is in the position of a subject or a son, has often, indeed, to do what he cannot but do. He is then occupied in the actual affairs and forgets his own life. What leisure has he for loving life and hating death? So, sir, you may proceed on your mission.

"I beg to tell you what I heard. In the intercourse between states, if they are near to each other, they can show mutual friendship with actual deeds. If they are far away, their good faith must be always renewed with oral messages. Messages will have to be transmitted by someone. But to transmit messages which express the delight or anger of two parties is the most difficult thing in the world. When the parties are delighted, their messages must be exaggerated with undue compliments. When they are angry, their messages must be exaggerated with undue condemnation. Exaggeration has the appearance of falsity. The appearance of falsity cannot command belief. When the appearance of falsity cannot command belief, the one who transmits the messages will suffer. Therefore, it is said in the 'Fa Yen': 'Transmit what the parties meant to say, but not the undue exaggerations.' Then one is likely to be safe.

"Moreover, skillful wrestlers begin with friendliness, but always end with antagonism. As their excitement grows excessive, their skill becomes extraordinary. Parties drinking according to ceremonies at first observe good order, but always end with confusion. As their excitement grows excessive, their fun becomes too noisy. So are all things. They begin with good faith, but end with contempt. They begin with the simple, but, as the ending is near, they become complex. Words are like wind and wave. Actions run the risk of actual loss. Wind and wave are easily set in motion. Risk can easily turn into real danger. Anger is chiefly caused by artful words and partial speeches. When people are angry, expressions of rage burst out like the inarticulate sounds emitted by an animal in the pangs of death. Their breath comes out quickly and is audible. Then animosities arise on both sides. For when one party drives the other too much into the corner, brute ideas are provoked without any one knowing how. If the agent does work without knowing how, who knows what will be the end? Therefore, in the 'Fa Yen,' it is said: 'Do not deviate from the original instruction you received. Do not urge on a settlement. To pass the limit is to go to excess!' To deviate from the original instruction and to urge on a settlement are dangerous. Satisfactory settlement is to be made with time. Dissatisfactory settlement, once made, is too late to be changed. Ought not one be careful? Let your mind make excursion with whatever may happen. Let yourself accept what is necessary and inevitable in order to cultivate your spirit. This is the perfect way. Why are you anxious about the answer of the other state? There is nothing better than to leave all to destiny, although this is not easy."

This story shows that in this world there are things which are inevitable, which we cannot but do. Let us be resigned to the inevitable. Let us be at ease in the face of anything that may happen. Let us leave all to destiny. It is also essential to forget one's own self. If one forgets one's own self, one would not love life, nor hate death. Worldly success or failure is of no importance. — *Tr.*

Yen Ho[1] was about to become tutor of the eldest son of Duke Ling of the state of Wei. Accordingly he consulted Chu Po Yu,[2] saying: "Here is a man whose disposition is naturally of a low order. If I allow him to proceed without principle, it will be at the peril of our state. If I insist on his proceeding according to principle, it will be at the peril of my own person. He has just enough wit to see the faults of others, but not his own. What am I to do in such a case?"

"A good question, indeed," replied Chu Po Yu. "You must be careful and begin with self-reformation. For your external bearing, there is nothing better than adaptation and conformation. For your inner mind, there is nothing better than peace and harmony. Yet in these there are two points to guard against. You must not let the external adaptation penetrate within, nor the inner harmony manifest itself without. In the former case, you will fall, you will ruin yourself, you will collapse, you will tumble.

You will be under the bad influence, and become a bad man yourself. — *Tr.*

"In the latter case, you will have reputation, you will have fame, you will be considered as a bogy, as a creature of evil omen.

You will be the object of others' envy. — *Tr.*

---

1 A scholar of the state of Lu.
2 A minister of the state of Wei.

72

"If the son of the prince should act as if he were a child, you also should act as if you were a child. If he should cast aside all differences, you should do the same. If he should cast aside all distinctions, you also should do the same. Then you can lead him to innocence.

"Do you not know the story of the mantis? In its rage it stretches out its arms to arrest the progress of a carriage, without knowing that it is not qualified. It thinks its ability is excellent. Be on your guard; be careful. If you always show your excellence to the son of the prince and thus offend him, probably you yourself will be in danger.

"Do you not know how the keeper of tigers do? He does not venture to give them living animals as food, for fear of exciting their fury when killing them. He does not venture to give them whole animals as food, for fear of exciting their fury when rending them. He knows when the tigers are hungry and when full; he understands the reason of their being angry. The tigers are of different species from man, yet they try to please their keeper. That is because he adapts himself to them. There are some who act against the nature of the tigers. These the tigers would kill.

"Those who are fond of horses use baskets and jars for receiving the dung and urine of the horses. Sometimes mosquitoes and gadflies light on them; and then, unexpectedly to the animal, the groom brushes them off. The result is that the horse breaks the bit and hurts the groom's head and chest. The groom intends to do something good; but in the end, what he intends to do is lost. Ought we not to be cautious?"

The best way to deal with man is to act in accordance with his nature. — *Tr.*

A master mechanic, called Shih, on his way to Chi, came to Chu Yuan. There he saw an oak tree, which was used as the altar of the land. The tree was so large that an ox standing behind it could not be seen. It measured a hundred spans around, and rose up to eighty cubits on the hill before it threw out any branches. Of the branches, there are ten or so, from each of which a boat could be hollowed out. People came to see it in crowds, as in a market place. But the master mechanic would not look at it, and went on without stopping. His disciples, however, looked at it till they were tired. Then they ran on to their master, and said to him: "Since we followed you with our axes and bills, we have never seen timber so good as this. Why, sir, did you not look at it? Instead, you went on without stopping!"

"Stop!" said the master mechanic. "That wood is useless. A boat made from it would sink, a coffin or shell would quickly rot, an article of furniture would soon go to pieces, a door would be covered with exuding sap, a pillar would be riddled with insects. It is useless and good for nothing. Therefore it has attained to so great an age."

When the master mechanic had come back, the altar tree appeared in his dream, saying: "With what other trees will you compare me? Will you compare me with the ornamental trees? There are hawthorns, pear trees, orange trees, pomelo trees, gourds, and others. The fruits are knocked down when they are ripe, and the trees are abused. The large branches are broken, and the smaller ones torn away. The life of these plants is suffering, because of their productive ability. They, therefore, cannot complete their natural term of existence, but come to a premature end in the middle of their time, and bring upon themselves destructive treatment from society. It is so with all things. For a long time I learned to be useless. There were several occasions on which I was nearly destroyed. Now I succeed in being useless, which is of the greatest use to me. If I am useful, could I have become so great? Moreover, you and I are both things; how can one thing pass judgment upon another? You are also a useless man and near death. How can you know the useless tree?"

When the master mechanic awoke, he told the dream to his disciples. "If its intention is to be useless, why does it serve as the altar for the spirit of the land?" asked the disciples.

"Be still," replied the master, "and do not say a word. The tree just pretends to be an altar. By so doing it can protect itself from the injury of those who do not know it is useless. If it were not an altar, it would be still in danger of being cut down. Moreover, what this tree maintains is different from what ordinary trees do. Therefore, to praise it with the conventional morality is far from the point."

Nan Po Tzu Chi, in loitering about the heights of Shang, saw a large and extraordinary tree. One thousand chariots might be sheltered under it, and its shade would cover them all. Tzu Chi said: "What tree is this? It must be a wonderful piece of timber!" When he looked up, however, at its smaller branches, they were twisted and crooked and could not be made into rafters and beams. When he looked down to its root, its stem was divided into many round portions, and neither coffin nor shell could be made from them. He licked one of its leaves, and his mouth felt torn and wounded. He smelled it, he became frantic, as if intoxicated, for more than three days. "This, indeed," said he, "is a tree good for nothing. It can thus become so great. Ah! the spiritual man lives with this kind of worthlessness."

In Sung there is the district of Chingshih. There catalpas, cypresses, and mulberry trees grow well. Those of them which are a span or two in circumference are cut down by persons who want to make posts to tie their monkeys. Those which are three or four spans round are cut down by those who want beams for their lofty houses. Those of seven or eight spans are cut down by noblemen and rich merchants who want single planks for the sides of coffins. In consequence, the trees cannot complete their natural term of life, but come to a premature end under ax and bill in the middle of their growth. This is the trouble of their worthiness.

In sacrifice, oxen that have white foreheads, pigs that have turned-up snouts, and men who are suffering from piles, cannot be used as offerings to the Yellow River. This all the wizards know. They consider these creatures as being unfortunate. But on this very account, the spiritual man considers them as being very fortunate.

There was a deformed man called Shu. His chin was hidden

in his navel. His shoulders were higher than the crown of his head. His spinal column pointed to the sky. The openings of his five viscera were all turned upward. His thigh bones were like ribs. By sharpening needles and washing clothes he was able to make a living. By sifting rice and cleaning it, he was able to support ten individuals. When the government was calling out soldiers, he wandered among them and there was no need to hide himself. When the government had any great service to be undertaken, because of his constant ailments, no work was assigned to him. When the government gave grain to the sick, he received three *chung* and ten bundles of firewood. If this man who was awkward in his bodily form was still able to make his living and complete his term of existence, how much more may he do who is awkward in his virtue?

> "The perfect man is useless to others, but everything is useful to itself. So the perfect man lets everything have its own achievement and name, while he himself is mingled with things without distinction. Therefore he is free from the harm of the human world, and always receives the real benefit. This is he who is awkward in his virtue."
> — *Kuo Hsiang.*

When Confucius went to Chu, Chieh Yu, the madman of Chu, wandered at his door, and said: "O Phoenix! O Phoenix! What can you do with this degenerated world? The future cannot be waited for; the past cannot be sought again. When good order prevails in the world, the sage seeks for accomplishment. When disorder prevails, he may preserve only his own life. At the present time, the best one can do is to escape from punishment. Happiness is lighter than a feather, but no one knows how to carry it. Calamity is heavier than the earth, and yet no one knows how to avoid it. Your approaching man with your virtue must stop, must stop. Your behaving with marked regulations is dangerous, is dangerous. I avoid notoriety, lest my path be injured. I walk crookedly, lest my feet be hurt. The mountain trees cause themselves to be cut. The grease causes itself to be fried. The cinnamon tree can be eaten, and therefore it is cut down. The varnish tree is useful, and therefore incisions are made in it. All men know the usefulness of the useful, but not that of the useless."

The useless trees are useless to others but free from harm. This is an example of the utility of the useless. Chuang Tzu, however, does not necessarily mean that every man should really be useless in the ordinary sense of the word. In the twentieth chapter, "The Mountain Tree," there is a story as follows:

"Chuang Tzu was walking on a mountain, when he saw a large tree with huge branches and luxuriant foliage. A woodcutter was resting by its side, but he would not touch it. When he was asked about the reason, he said that it was good for nothing. Then Chuang Tzu said: 'This tree, because of its uselessness, is able to complete its natural term of existence.' Having left the mountain, Chuang Tzu lodged in the house of his friend. The friend was glad and ordered his waiting lad to kill a goose and boil it. The lad said: 'One of our geese can cackle, and the other cannot; which of them shall I kill?' The host said: 'Kill the one that cannot cackle.'

"Next day, his disciple asked Chuang Tzu, saying: 'Yesterday we saw the mountain tree that can complete its natural term of existence, because of its uselessness. Now for the same reason, our host's goose died. Which of these positions would you, Master, prefer to be in?'

"Chuang Tzu laughed and said: 'I would prefer to be in a position which is between the useful and the useless. This seems to be the right position, but is really not so. Therefore it would not put me beyond trouble. But he who makes excursion in *Tao* and *Te* is not exposed to any trouble. He is above the reach to both praise and detraction, now like a dragon, now like a snake. He changes · with time and has no insistence. He is now high and now low, taking harmony as the measure. He enjoys himself at ease with the author of things. He treats things as things, and is not being treated as a thing by them. What can involve him in trouble?'"

This recalls to us what is said in the first chapter. The perfect man depends upon nothing, and makes excursion in the infinite. "The perfect has no self; the spiritual man has no achievement; the sage has no name." They are so because they let everything do its own work according to its own ability, and have its own name. Since they are so, they always are, or seem to be, of no utility, of no distinction. Because of this, they are free from all trouble. As Kuo Hsiang said: "This is he who is awkward in his virtue." This is the great utility of the useless.

The last story of this chapter shows the danger of showing one's own excellence to others, of trying to right others with one's own standard. When the world is in peace, let it alone. When the world is in disorder, let it alone also. People can work out their own salvation. If one does not act according to this principle, but tries to insist on his own standard, and to correct others artificially with it, then one will certainly get in trouble. Yet that is what people usually do, because they "know the utility of the useful, but not that of the useless."—*Tr.*

CHAPTER V
THE EVIDENCE OF VIRTUE
COMPLETE

The main purpose of this chapter is to show what complete virtue is and how great is its influence. — *Tr.*

In the state of Lu, there was a man, named Wang Tai, who had lost one of his feet. His followers were as numerous as those of Confucius. Chang Chi asked Confucius, saying: "Wang Tai is one who has been mutilated. Yet he divides with you, sir, the teaching of the state of Lu. He neither preaches, nor discusses. Yet those who go to him are empty, but those who come back are full. Is there, indeed, such a thing as instruction without words? While the body is deformed, may the mind be perfect? What sort of man is he?"

"This master is a sage," replied Confucius. "I myself did not go to him, simply because I am late. I myself will make him my master, to say nothing of those who are not equal to me. I will lead the whole world to follow him, to say nothing of the state of Lu."

"He is a man," said Chang Chi, "who has been mutilated, yet is superior to you. He must be very different from the ordinary man. What is the peculiar way in which his mind functions?"

"Death and life are great considerations," said Confucius, "yet neither can affect him. Though heaven and earth were to be overturned and to fall, he would remain unmoved. He sees clearly the most perfect and is not affected by things. He knows that the evolution of things is due to destiny and thus he keeps the essential."

"What do you mean?" asked Chang Chi.

"If we see things from the point of view of their difference," said Confucius, "even liver and gall are as far away from each other as Chu from Yueh. If we see things from the point of view of their identity, all things are one. The latter viewpoint is what this man takes. So he knows not even to what his ears and eyes are appropriate, but dallies with the harmony of virtue. He sees the unity of things, but not his own loss. He considers the loss of his foot just as the falling of so much earth."

"In the cultivation of himself," said Chang Chi, "with knowledge he attained the mind. With mind he attained the eternal mind. But why have things gathered around him?"

"Men do not seek to see themselves in running water," said Confucius, "but in still water. Only what is still can gather things together. Of those who receive the influence of earth, only pine and cypress are green both in winter and summer. Of those who received the influence of heaven, only Shun was correct. Fortunately, he could correct his own life, and then the lives of others. By preservation of the original strength and by elimination of fear, a single brave man may fight his way successfully through nine armies. If such a result can be achieved by this brave man, who can sacrifice himself in search of fame, how much more by one who would control heaven and earth and embrace all things, who considers his body as a temporary lodging, and ears and eyes as mere images, who unifies all that knowledge knows, and whose mind never dies. He would choose a day on which he would ascend afar, and people would follow him. How does he care about worldly affairs?"

Shen Tu Chia was a man who had lost one of his feet. He studied under Po Hun Wu Jen with Tzu Chan of the state of Cheng. The latter said to him: "If I should leave here first, will you please remain awhile? If you should leave here first, I will remain behind."

Tzu Chan, being the prime minister of the state, was ashamed to walk along with the mutilated man. — *Tr.*

Next day they were again sitting together on the same mat in the hall. Tzu Chan said: "If I should leave here first, will you please remain awhile? If you should leave here first, I will remain. Now I am about to go. Will you remain or not? Moreover, when you see a minister of state, you do not try to get out of his way. Do you consider yourself equal to him?"

"In the school of our master," said Shen Tu Chia, "could there be such a minister of state? You are one who is proud of his rank and thinks he is superior to the rest. I heard that, if a mirror is perfectly bright, dust and dirt will not collect on it; if they do, the mirror is not bright. He who associates for long with the wise will be without fault. Now the wise man you have chosen to make you great is our master. Yet you can utter words like these. Is not this your fault?"

"You have been what you are," said Tzu Chan, "yet you still attempt to emulate the goodness of Yao. Would an estimate of your virtue not sufficiently lead you to an examination of yourself?"

"Those who make themselves notorious," said Shen Tu Chia, "and think they ought to lose nothing, are many in number. But those who do not make themselves notorious and think they ought to keep nothing, are few. To recognize the inevitable and quietly to acquiesce in it as the appointment of destiny are the achievement of the virtuous alone. When men are wandering within the range of Yi's[1] arrow, the middle of the field is the place where they would be hit. If they are not hit, that is destiny.

"Because of the conflict of their interest, men always struggle among themselves. Therefore, in the world of men, Yi is everywhere. With the exception of those who, having no self and knowledge, simply follow the nature of things, everyone is in the range of Yi.'s arrow.... Whether one is hit or not, only destiny can determine. Everyone is in some situation, but not everyone knows that every situation is destined. Therefore those who are not hit, consider themselves as specially skillful, and are thus much delighted. But at other times when they are hit, they regret their mistakes and thus hurt their spirit. That is because they know nothing about destiny. We have our life, not because we wish to have it. Then within our life, a span of one hundred years, sitting, rising, walking, standing, acting, resting, gaining, losing, feeling, instinct, knowledge, and ability, all that we have, all that we have not, all that we do, and all that we meet, are not so because we want them. By natural reason, they are what they are. Yet there are many who are sentimental towards these. They are thus against nature and mistaken." — *Kuo Hsiang.*

---

1 A famous archer of antiquity.

"Those who have two feet and laugh at me for having but one foot, are many. I used to be very angry at them. But since I came to our master, I have ceased to be troubled about it. It may be that our master has purified me with the good. I have been with him for nineteen years without being aware of the loss of my foot. Now you and I are making excursion in the inner world, yet you always direct your attention to my external body. Are you not wrong in this?"

Tzu Chan felt uneasy, changed the expression of his countenance, and said: "Sir, I beg you to say no more about it."

There was a man of the state of Lu, who had been mutilated and was called Shu Shan the Toeless. Walking on his heels, he went to see Confucius. The latter said: "You were not careful and so brought such a misfortune upon yourself. Now it is too late for you to come to see me."

"Through my ignorance of the proper way and taking too little care of my body," said the Toeless, "I came to lose my foot. Now I come to you, I still possess what is more valuable than my foot, and which, therefore, I am anxious to preserve entire. There is nothing that heaven does not cover; there is nothing that earth does not sustain. I thought you, sir, would be as heaven and earth, and did not expect you to receive me in such a way."

"I am stupid," said Confucius. "Why do you not come in, so I can tell you what I have learned?"

When the Toeless went away, Confucius said: "You disciples should be encouraged by this. This toeless one has been mutilated. Yet he still is anxious to learn how to make up the evil of his former conduct, how much more should those do so whose virtue is entire!"

The Toeless went to see Lao Tzu, and said: "I think Confucius is not yet a perfect man. Why does he so often imitate you? He is seeking for the reputation of being extraordinary and marvelous, without knowing that the perfect man considers this as handcuffs and fetters?"

"Why did you not lead him to see that life and death are one," said Lao Tzu, "and that the right and the wrong are the

84

same, thus freeing him from his handcuffs and fetters?"

"He is receiving natural penalty," said the Toeless. "How can he be freed?"

Duke Ai, of the state of Lu, asked Confucius, saying: "There was an ugly man in the state of Wei, named Ai Tai To. The men who lived with him thought of him so much that they could not be away from him. Of the women who had seen him, ten and more said to their parents: 'I would rather be his concubine than to be another man's wife.' He was never heard to lead in anything; he just followed others. He had not the position of a ruler, so as to be able to save men from death. He had no revenue, so as to be able to fill men's stomachs. Moreover, he was ugly enough to scare the whole world. He followed others and never led them. His knowledge did not go beyond his immediate neighbourhood. Yet both men and women congregated around him. He must be different from the ordinary men. I sent for him and saw that he was certainly ugly enough to scare the whole world. When he had lived with me less than one month, I began to pay attention to his personality. Before he had lived with me a full year, I trusted him thoroughly. As my state wanted a prime minister, I offered him the government. He responded to my proposal quietly and indifferently, as if he would decline it. I was ashamed of myself, and finally gave the government to his hand. In a short time he left me and went away. I was sorry and felt that I had sustained a loss, as if there was no one to share the pleasure of the state. What sort of man is he?"

"Once when I was on a mission to the state of Chu," said Confucius, "I saw some young pigs sucking at their dead mother. After a while, startling at her, they all went away. They felt that she did not see them and was no longer like themselves. What they loved in their mother was not the body, but that which made the body what it was. When a man dies in battle, he is buried without military decorations. When a man has no feet, he does not care about shoes. In each case they have lost the fundamentals. The wives of the king do not cut their nails, or pierce their ears. When a man is newly married, he remains outside the court and is free from his official duties. A perfect body can achieve some result; how much more does he achieve, who has perfect virtue? Now Ai Tai To said nothing, but was believed. He did nothing, but was loved. He caused a man to offer him the government, and was only afraid that he would not accept. He must be a man whose character is perfect, and whose virtue unmanifested."

"What is meant by perfect character?" asked Duke Ai.

Confucius said: "Death and life, existence and peril, ill and good fortune, wealth and poverty, worth and worthlessness, praise and blame, hunger and thirst, cold and hot — these are changes of events and the operation of destiny. They succeed one another like the alternation of day and night; knowledge knows not where they begin. One should not allow such things to disturb one's harmony. One should not allow such things to enter one's mind. One's mind must be harmonious, content, and complete. One must always be cheerful, and kind with things. The mind is following the changes of events. This is called the perfect character."

"What is meant by unmanifested virtue?"

"Perfect balance is the virtue of still water," said Confucius. "This is the model for us. The inner peace is preserved and no disturbance is received from without. Virtue is the perfect attainment of harmony. The perfect man has virtue, but looks as if he had not. Such a man is indispensable to all things."

Some day afterwards, Duke Ai related this conversation to Ming Tzu[1] and said: "Formerly when I sat on the throne to rule the world, held the reins, and took care of the people, I thought that is the most perfect. Now when I heard the sayings of the perfect man, I am afraid that I have no real virtue, and that, by using myself too lightly, I may ruin my state. Confucius and I are not prince and subject, but merely friends in virtue."

A man who had no lips, whose legs were bent so that he could only walk on his toes, addressed his counsels to Duke Ling of

_____
1 One of the disciples of Confucius.

86

Wei. The duke was so pleased with him that he looked on a well-formed man as having too lean and too small a neck. Another man who had a goiter as large as a big jar, addressed his counsel to Duke Huan of Chi. The duke was so pleased with him that he looked on a well-formed man as having too lean and too small a neck.

These show that when one's virtue is excellent, any deficiency in bodily form may be forgotten. When men do not forget what they ought to forget, but forget what they ought not, we have a case of real oblivion.

The sage, therefore, has another place for his excursion. He considers knowledge as a curse, convention as glue, morality as the art of human intercourse, arts as belonging to the same category as commerce. He makes no plan, and therefore needs no knowledge. He does not divide things, and therefore needs no glue. He has no deficiency in his character, and therefore needs no morality. He does not want any merchandise, and therefore needs no commerce. In these four ways he is nourished by nature. To be nourished by nature is to be fed by nature. Since he is fed by nature, what is the use of art? He has human form, but no human affection. Since he has human form, he is a man among men. Since he has no human affection, he is above the ordinary distinction of right and wrong. Insignificant and small is that by which he belongs to humanity. Grand and great is he in his unique identification with nature.

Hui Tzu asked Chuang Tzu, saying: "Are there men who have no affections?"

"Yes," said Chuang Tzu.

"If a man has no affection," said Hui Tzu, "how can he be called a man at all?"

"*Tao* gives him the appearance," said Chuang Tzu, "and nature gives him the form. How can he not be called a man?"

"Since he is called a man," said Hui Tzu, "how can he be without affections?"

"That is not what I mean by affection," said Chuang Tzu. "When I say a man is without affection, I mean one who does not inflict internal injury upon himself with desires and aversions, who is always in accordance with nature, and does nothing to increase artificially what is already in his life."

"If he does nothing to increase what is already in his life," said Hui Tzu, "how can he maintain it?"

"*Tao* gives him the appearance," said Chuang Tzu, "and nature gives him the form. He does not inflict any internal injury upon himself. But you devote yourself to the external, and wear out your vitality. You prop yourself against a tree and mutter, or lean over a table and sleep. Nature chose for you your bodily form, and you babble with the discussion of 'the hard and the white.'"

CHAPTER VI
THE GREAT TEACHER

This chapter gives a description of the perfect man, or the "true man," who can be the great teacher of the world. — *Tr.*

He who knows the work of nature and the work of man is usually considered as perfect. He who knows the work of nature will live in accordance with nature. He who knows the work of man will nourish what is unknown to his knowledge with what is known.

What is unknown to knowledge is the work of nature, such as the circulation of blood, the working of the bodily inner organs, etc. What is known to knowledge is the work of man, such as reading, writing, etc. — *Tr.*

He thus can complete his natural term of years and does not come to an untimely end in the middle of his term of life. This is knowledge at its best.

Yet there is still some trouble. Here one had to be dependent upon something, which is knowledge, and knowledge is far from certainty. How does one know that what one calls nature is not man and what one calls man is not nature?

Whenever there is knowledge, there is confusion. The best way is to transcend knowledge. This has been fully discussed in the second chapter. The true knowledge of the true man is the knowledge of what we call pure experience. This can be seen in the following description of the true man. — *Tr.*

The true man only has true knowledge. What is a true man? The true man of old did not oppose even the minority. He did not seek for heroic accomplishment. He laid no plans. Therefore, he had neither regret in failure, nor self-complacency in success. Thus he could scale heights without fear, enter water without being wet, and fire without feeling hot. Such is he whose knowledge has ascended to *Tao*.

The true man of old slept without dreaming and waked without anxiety. He ate without discrimination, breathing deep breaths. The breaths of the true man come from his heels, while men generally breathe from their throats. Out of the men who are defeated, words are retched up like vomit.

The true man is quiet, calm, and tranquil, while men in general are always in a state of confusion and disturbance. — *Tr.*

If a man's lusts and desires are deep, his spring of nature is shallow.

The true man of old knew neither to love life, nor to hate death. Living, he felt no elation; dying, he offered no resistance. Unconsciously he went; unconsciously he came; that was all. He did not try consciously to forget what his beginning had been, or to seek what his end would be. He received with delight anything that came to him, and left without consciousness anything that he had forgotten. He did not prefer the conscious mind to *Tao*, or to supplement nature with man. Such was what we call the true man.

Being such, his mind was free from all thoughts. [1] His demeanour was still and silent. His forehead beamed with simplicity. He was cold as autumn, and warm as spring. His joy and anger occurred as naturally as the four seasons. He was in harmony with all things without knowledge of any fixed standard. Therefore, the sage, in his conduct of war, might destroy a country without losing the affection of the people. His benefits might extend to ten thousand generations without his being a lover of man.

Therefore, he who purposely seeks to know all things is not a sage. He who purposely manifests affection is not a man of benevolence. He who purposely observes the changes of time is not a man of wisdom. He who cannot unify the beneficial and the harmful is not a man of virtue. He who acts for fame and

---

1 Reading 志 as 忘.

thus loses his own nature is not a man of learning. He who loses his own nature and thus misses the true way cannot be independent of others. Such men as Hu Pu Chieh, Wu Kuang, Po Yi, Shu Chi, Chi Tzu, Hsu Yu, Chi To, Shen Tu Ti —

All were moralists of the ancient times. — *Tr.*

all acted according to the standard of others, but not to their own nature; all worked for the delight of others, but not for that of themselves.

The appearance of the true man of old was like something that is lofty, [1] but with no danger of a downfall, [2] something that seems to be insufficient but has no need of addition. He acts [3] independently, [4] but is not severe. His emptiness was manifest, yet there was no display. He was smiling, and seemed to be pleased. He responded spontaneously, as if there were no choice. His accumulated attractiveness appeared in his expression. His blankness fixed man's attachment to his virtue. His broadness [5] had the appearance of pride. [6] His loftiness seemed to be uncontrollable. His mystery seemed to be unknowable. Being always unconscious, he forgot what to say. He considered law as the outward manifestation of government, ceremony as the wings, knowledge as the requirement of time, and virtue as the guide. To consider law as the outward manifestation of government means flexibility of punishment. To consider ceremony as the wings means that it is the usage of the world of men. To consider knowledge as the requirement of time means to follow the inevitable course of things. To consider virtue as the guide means to return to the former home

Nature. — *Tr.*

with those who can walk. Thus he acts spontaneously, yet people

---

1 Reading 義 as 峨, according to Yu Yueh.
2 Reading 朋 as 崩, according to Yu Yueh.
3 Reading 與 as 趣, according to Li Chen.
4 Reading 觚 as 孤, according to Li Chen.
5 Reading 厲 as 廣, according to the "Shi Wen."
6 Reading 世 as 泰, according to Yu Yueh.

think it was with special effort. In this way what he liked was reduced to one. What he did not like was also reduced to one. That which is one is one. That which is not one is also one. He who knows the one is the follower of nature. He who knows not is the follower of man. Neither nature nor man should overthrow the other. This is the true man.

> "The true man unifies nature and man, and equalizes all things. To him, there is no mutual opposition in all things. There is no mutual conquest of nature and man. Therefore, he is empty and is everything. He is unconscious and is everywhere. He thus mysteriously unifies his own self with its other." — *Kuo Hsiang.*

> This is what Chuang Tzu called "taking two courses at once," as mentioned in the second chapter. — *Tr.*

Life and death are the appointment of destiny. Their sequence, like the succession of day and night, is the evolution of nature. There is something which is beyond the interference of man. Such is the reality of things. There are those who regard heaven as their father and still love it; — how much more should they love that which is greater than heaven!

> *Tao.—Tr.*

There are those who regard their ruler as superior to themselves and would sacrifice their lives for him; — how much more should they do so for that which is more real than the ruler!

> *Tao.* — *Tr.*

When the springs are dried up, the fishes crowd together on the land. They moisten each other with the dampness about them, and keep one another wet by their slime.

> The moralists who reform the world with benevolence and righteousness. — *Tr.*

94

But it is better for them to forget each other in rivers and lakes.

Men forget each other in *Tao*. —*Tr.*

People praise Yao and condemn Chieh, but it is better for them to forget both and to assimilate their different ways.

The universe carries us in our bodies, toils us through our life, gives us repose with our old age, and rests us in our death. That which makes our life a good makes our death a good also. A boat may be stored in a creek; a net [1] may be stored in a lake; these may be said to be safe enough. But at midnight a strong man may come and carry them away on his back. The ignorant do not see that no matter how well you store things, smaller ones in larger ones, there will always be a chance for them to be lost. But if you store the universe in the universe, there will be no room left for it to be lost. This is the great truth of things. To have attained to the human form is a source of joy. But, in the infinite evolution, there are thousands of other forms that are equally good. What an incomparable bliss it is to undergo these countless transitions! Therefore the sages makes excursions into that which cannot be lost, and together with it he remains.

"The sages make excursion on the road of evolution, and follow the stream of daily renovation. Things change, the sages change with them. Change is infinite, the sages are infinite also. They lose in life, but endure in death. So they endure always." — *Kuo Hsiang.*

Those who consider early death, old age, beginning, and end, as equally good, are to be followed by others; — how much more is that, to which all things belong, and upon which the great evolution depends!

This passage shows that the excursion of the true man really depends upon nothing, as was mentioned in the first chapter. — *Tr.*

Tao has reality and evidence, but no action and form. It may be transmitted, but cannot be received. It may be attained,

---

1 Reading 山 as 汕, according to Yu Yueh.

but cannot be seen. It exists by and through itself. It exists prior to heaven and earth, and indeed for all eternity. It causes the gods to be divine and the world to be produced.

> "*Tao* does not cause the gods to be divine, but they are divine themselves. So *Tao* causes them to be divine by not causing them. *Tao* does not produce the world, but the world produces itself. So *Tao* produces it by not producing it." — *Kuo Hsiang.*

It is above the zenith, but it is not high. It is beneath the nadir, but it is not low. It is prior to heaven and earth, but it is not ancient. It is older than the most ancient, but it is not old.

> "This shows that *Tao* is everywhere. Therefore, it is in the highest place, but it is not high. It is in the lowest place, but it is not low. It is in ancient times, but it itself is not ancient. It is in old age, but it itself is not old. It is everywhere, but everywhere it is nothing." — *Kuo Hsiang.*

Hsi Wei attained it, and with it he adjusted heaven and earth. Fu Hsi attained it, and with it he penetrated to the origin of matter. The Great Bear attained it, and so it has never erred from its course. The sun and moon attained it, and so they have never ceased their motion. Kan Pi[1] attained it, and with it he entered the Kunlun Mountains. Feng Yi[1] attained it, and with it he made excursion to the Great River. Chien Wu attained it, and with it he dwelt on Mount Tai. The Yellow Emperor[2] attained it, and with it he ascended the cloudy heaven. Chuan Hsu[2] attained it, and with it he dwelt in the Dark Palace. Yu Chiang[3] attained it, and so he was set on the north pole. Hsi Wang Mu[3] attained it, and so she was given her seat on Shaokuang Mountain; no one knows her beginning, no one knows her end. Peng Tsu attained it, and so he lived from the time of Shun to that of the Five Princes. Fu

---

1 A spirit of the mountains and rivers.
2 A legendary ruler.
3 A legendary spirit.

Yueh [1] attained it, and with it he became the prime minister of Wu Ting [2] and controlled the whole empire. Then, charioting upon one constellation and drawn by another, he made himself equal to the stars of heaven.

This passage gives a poetic description of *Tao* and those who attained it. — *Tr.*

Nan Po Tzu Kuei asked Nu Chu, saying: "You are old, sir, but your countenance is like that of a child. How is this?"

"I have become acquainted with *Tao*," replied Nu Chu.

"Can I learn *Tao*?" asked Nan Po Tzu Kuei.

"No, how can you?" replied Nu Chu. "You are not the man to do so. There was Pu Liang Yi, who had the genius of a sage, but not the *Tao*. I have the *Tao*, but not the genius. I wished to teach him, so he might really become a sage. To teach the *Tao* of a sage to a man who has the genius, seems to be an easy matter. But no, I kept on telling him; after three days, he began to be able to disregard all worldly matters. After his having disregarded all worldly matters, I kept on telling him; after seven days, he began to be able to disregard all external things. After his having disregarded all external things, I kept on telling him; after nine days, he began to be able to disregard his own existence. Having disregarded his own existence, he was enlightened. Having become enlightened, he then was able to gain the vision of the One. Having the vision of the One, he then was able to transcend the distinction of past and present. Having transcended the distinction of past and present, he was then able to enter the realm where life and death are no more. Then, to him, the destruction of life did not mean death, nor the prolongation of life an addition to the duration of his existence. He would follow anything; he would receive anything. To him, everything was in destruction, everything was in construction. This is called tranquillity in disturbance. Tranquillity in disturbance means perfection."

---

1 A minister of the Shang Dynasty.
2 A king of the Shang Dynasty.

"That is, in spite of his spiritual condition as above described, he still adapted himself naturally to life among his fellow men. The retirement of a hermit is by no means necessary to the perfection of the pure man." — *Giles.*

"Where did you learn this?" asked Nan Po Tzu Kuei.

"I learned it from writing," replied Nu Chu, "writing from learning, learning from understanding, understanding from maintaining, maintaining from application, application from enjoyment, enjoyment from mystery, mystery from namelessness, namelessness from infinity."

This story describes the procedure in the attainment of *Tao.* — *Tr.*

Tzu Ssu, Tzu Yu, Tzu Li, Tzu Lai, said to each other: "Whosoever can make nothing the head of his existence, life its backbone, and death its tail, whosoever knows that death and life, existence and nonexistence, are one — that man shall be our friend. The four men smiled, silently agreed with each other, and thus became friends.

Not long after, Tzu Yu fell ill, and Tzu Ssu went to see him. "Great is the Maker of things! He caused me to have such a deformed manner," said the sick man. His back was hunched; his viscera were at the top of his body; his cheeks were level with his navel; his shoulders were higher than his crown; his neck vertebral bones pointed to the sky: the principles of his whole body were out of order. Nevertheless, his mind was at ease and not affected. He limped to a well, looked at his reflection, and said: "Alas! the Maker of things has caused me to have such a deformed appearance!"

"Do you dislike it?" asked Tzu Ssu.

"No," said Tzu Yu, "why should I dislike it? If my left arm would be transformed into a cock, I should mark with it the time of night. If my right arm would be transformed into a crossbow, I should look for a bird to bring down and roast. If my rump bone would be transformed into a wheel, and my spirit

98

into a horse, I should mount it, and would have no need of any other steed. When we come, it is because we have the occasion to be born. When we go, we simply follow the natural course. Those who are quiet at the proper occasion and follow the course of nature cannot be affected by sorrow and joy. These men were considered by the ancients as people who are released from bondage. Those who cannot release themselves are hedged in with the trammels of things. Moreover, that the individual things cannot overcome nature is a long-acknowledged fact. Why should I dislike my condition?"

By and by, Tzu Lai fell ill, and laid gasping at the point of death, while his wife and children wept around him. Tzu Li went to see him, and said to the wife and children: "Go, hush, get out of the way. Do not disturb the natural evolution." Then, leaning against the door, he said: "Great is nature! What will she make of you? Will she make you into the liver of a rat? Will she make you into the arm of an insect?"

"Wherever a parent tells a son to go," replied Tzu Lai, "east, west, south, or north, he simply follows the command. Nature, the Yin and Yang, is no other than a man's parent. If she bid me die quickly, and I demur, then I am obstinate and rebellious; she does no wrong. The universe carries me in my body, toils me through my life, gives me repose with old age, and rests me in death. What makes my life a good makes my death a good also. Here is a great foundryman, casting his metal. If the metal should leap up and say: 'I must be made into a sword, Mo Yeh',[1] the great foundryman would certainly regard it as uncanny. Now if I, who once meet[2] the human form, were to say: 'I must be a man, I must be a man,' the Maker of things would certainly regard me as uncanny. If we take the universe as a great melting pot, and nature as a great foundryman, what place is it not right for us to go? Calmly we die; quietly we live."

This story is a concrete illustration of the theory of hiding the

---

1 Name of a famous sword.
2 Reading 犯 as 逢 according to Chang Ping-ling.

universe within the universe, and of the independence of the perfect man which was mentioned in the first chapter. — *Tr.*

Tzu Sang Hu, Meng Tzu Fan, and Tzu Chin Chang were friends. They said to each other: "Who can associate in nonassociation, and cooperate in noncooperation? Who can mount to heaven and roaming through the clouds, disporting in the infinite and become oblivious of existence, forever and ever without end?" The three men looked at each other and smiled, silently agreed one with another, and thus became friends.

Shortly afterwards, Tzu Sang Hu died. Before he was buried, Confucius heard of the event, and sent Tzu Kung[1] to take part in the mourning. But Tzu Kung found that one of the friends composed a song, and the other was playing on the lute. They sang together in unison: "Alas! Sang Hu! Alas! Sang Hu! you have returned to the real, but we still remain here as men, alas!"

Tzu Kung hurried in and said: "I venture to ask whether it is decorous to sing in the presence of the corpse."

The two men looked at each other, laughed, and said: "What does this man know about the idea of decorum?"

Tzu Kung went back and told Confucius, asking him: "What sort of men are those? They have no culture and consider their body as external to themselves. They sing in the presence of the corpse, without a change of countenance. I do not know what to call them. What sort of men are they?"

"They travel outside the human world," said Confucius. "I travel within it. There is no common ground for these two ways; I was wrong in sending you there to mourn. They are companions[2] of the Maker of things, and make excursion with the unity of the universe. They consider life as an appendage attached to them, an excrescence annexed to them. They consider death as a separation of the appendage, and a dispersion of the excrescence. With these views, how can they be aware of the

---

1 One of the disciples of Confucius.
2 Reading 人 as 偶, according to Wang Yin-chih.

superiority of life and the inferiority of death? They consider their body as a composition of different borrowed elements. They just temporarily lodge within it. They forget their liver and gall, and ignore their ears and eyes. They end and they begin without knowing either the beginning or the end. Unconsciously, they stroll beyond the dirty world and wander in the realm of nonaction. How can they foolishly trouble themselves with conventionalities simply for the sake of ordinary people?"

"If such is the case," said Tzu Kung, "why should you, Master, stick to the conventionalities?"

"I am nature's condemned one," said Confucius. "However, that is what we are in common."

"I venture to ask you to give further explanation," said Tzu Kung.

"Fishes enjoy water; men enjoy *Tao*," said Confucius. "Enjoying water, the fishes cleave the pools, and their nourishment is thus adequate. Enjoying *Tao*, men do nothing and their life is thus self-sufficient. [1] Hence it is said: 'Fishes forget one another in rivers and lakes; men forget one another in *Tao*.' "

"May I ask about the abnormal man?" said Tzu Kung.

"The abnormal man is abnormal to man but is normal with nature," said Confucius. "Therefore, it is said: 'The inferior man for nature is a superior man among men; the superior man for nature is an inferior man among men.' " [2]

Yen Hui asked Confucius, saying: "When Meng Sun Tsai's mother died, he wept without sniveling, his heart felt no distress. During the period of mourning, he exhibited no sorrow. Although wanting in these points, yet he was considered as the best mourner in the state of Lu. Without reality, can one get the reputation? I am astonished at this."

"Meng Sun is perfect," said Confucius. "He is more advanced than knowledge. Some people compare life with death, and cannot see the difference between them. This is good, but there is still the comparison. Meng Sun does not know what life is or

---

1 Reading 定 as 足, according to Yu Yueh.
2 The text of this sentence is rearranged according to Wang Hsien-chien.

what death is. He knows neither to prefer the one, nor the other. He simply follows the transformation, and awaits the occurrence yet unknown. Moreover, we are now in transformation, how do we know what has not yet occurred? We are now transforming into what has not yet occurred, how do we know what has occurred already? May be you and I are in a dream, from which we have not yet awaked. To Meng Sun, there is a transformation of form, but no trouble in the mind; there is a change [1] of lodging, but no real death. He wept; he simply followed the example of others. He would consider everything as his own self, how can he know that there is something which, among others, is particularly called his own self? You dream that you are a bird, and soar to the sky. You dream that you are a fish, and dive into the water. We cannot tell whether the speaker now is awake or is dreaming. A happy feeling is prior to smiling. A forced smile is not natural. Resting in the natural and going with the process of evolution, you will enter into the empty, the natural, and the one."

Yi Erh Tzu went to see Hsu Yu. Hsu Yu said: "How has Yao benefited you?"

"Yao said to me," replied Yi Erh Tzu, "that I must practise benevolence and righteousness, and distinguish clearly between the right and the wrong."

"Then, what do you want here?" said Hsu Yu. "If Yao had already branded you with the practice of benevolence and righteousness, and cut off your nose with the distinction of the right and the wrong, how would you be able to wander on the road of freedom and ease, of aimless and unregulated enjoyment, and of ever-changing evolution?"

"That may be," said Yi Erh Tzu, "but I should like to skirt along its hedges."

"No," said Hsu Yu, "when a man is blind, he has nothing to do with the appreciation of the beauty of human form, or of the charm of colours."

"Wu Chuang's disregard of her beauty," said Hsu Yu, "Chu

---

1 Reading 且 as 徂, according to Chang Ping-ling.

Liang's disregard of his strength, the Yellow Emperor's abandonment of his knowledge — all these were brought about by a process of filing and hammering. How do you know that the Maker of things may not obliterate the marks of my branding, and supply my dismemberment, so that, again perfect in my form, I may follow you as my teacher?"

"Ah!" said Hsu Yu, "that cannot yet be known. But I shall just give you an outline. O my master! O my master! He tears all things into pieces, yet he is not just. His blessing reaches all generation, yet he is not benevolent. He is more ancient than the highest antiquity, yet he is not old. He covers heaven, supports earth, and fashions the various forms of all things, yet he is not skillful. In him I make an excursion."

> This passage gives a description of the nature of *Tao*. *Tao* just lets everything do its own work. Its success or failure are the results of its own work. It is because of this that *Tao* is said to be doing everything by doing nothing. — *Tr.*

"I have made some progress," said Yen Hui.
"What do you mean?" asked Confucius.
"I have forgotten human-heartedness and righteousness," replied Yen Hui.
"Very well, but that is not enough," said Confucius.
Another day Yen Hui again saw Confucius and said: "I have made some progress."
"What do you mean?" asked Confucius.
"I have forgotten rituals and music," replied Yen Hui.
"Very well, but that is not enough," said Confucius.
Another day Yen Hui again saw Confucius and said: "I have made some progress."
"What do you mean?" asked Confucius.
"I sit in forgetfulness," replied Yen Hui.
At this Confucius changed countenance and asked: "What do you mean by sitting in forgetfulness?"
To which Yen Hui replied: "My limbs are nerveless and my intelligence is dimmed. I have abandoned my body and

103

discarded my knowledge. Thus I become one with the infinite. This is what I mean by sitting in forgetfulness."

"If you have become one with the infinite," said Confucius, "you have no personal likes and dislikes. If you have become one with the Great Evolution, you are one who merely follow its changes. If you really have achieved this, I should like to follow your steps."

Another description of the state of pure experience. — *Tr.*

Tzu Yu and Tzu Sang were friends. Once when it had rained for ten days, Tzu Yu said: "I fear that Tzu Sang may be in distress." So he packed up some food and went to feed him. Arriving at the door, he heard some sort of utterance between singing and wailing, accompanied with the sound of a lute, as follows:

"O father! O mother! O nature! O man!" It seemed that the voice could hardly sustain itself, and the line was hurriedly pronounced. Tzu Yu entered and said: "Why are you singing in such a manner?"

"I am trying to think," said Tzu Sang, "who have brought me to such an extremity. But I think in vain. My father and mother would hardly wish me to be poor. Heaven covers all things equally; earth supports all things equally. How could they make me in particular poor? I am asking to know who it is, but without success. It is, then, destiny that has brought me to such an extremity."

CHAPTER VII
THE PHILOSOPHER-KING

"Until, then, philosophers are kings, or the kings and princes of this world have the spirit and power of philosophy, and political greatness and wisdom meet in one, . . . cities will never cease from ill — no, nor the human race, as I believe — and then only will our state have a possibility of life and behold the light of day." This was the ideal of Plato, and also of most Chinese philosophers. It seems that the titles and the order of the seven "inner chapters" of the *Chuang-tzu* also bear this significance. The first chapter describes the state of absolute freedom; the second, the state of absolute equality. He who attains these states can cultivate his own life and live with others in the human world. His virtue is complete, and with it he naturally influences the people. He thus becomes the great teacher, and the great teacher should also be king. "Political greatness" should be the crown of "wisdom." Philosophy should be sagely in principle and kingly in practice. — *Tr.*

Yeh Chueh interviewed Wang Yi. He asked four questions, but Wang Yi answered none of them. On this Yeh Chueh was very delighted; by leaps and bounds, he went off and told Pu Yi Tzu.

"Did you not know this before?" said Pu Yi Tzu. "Emperor Shun was not equal to Emperor Tai. [1] Shun still kept benevolence to oblige men. He did win them. But in his mind, there is still the distinction of what was man and what was not, and he never rose above the distinction. Emperor Tai would sleep in tranquillity, and awake in contented simplicity. At one time, he would think himself a horse; at another, an ox. His knowledge was true, his virtue genuine, and he never sank to the distinction of what was man and what was not."

This story shows that in the world of nondistinction, Taoism has its golden time. — *Tr.*

---

1 A legendary ruler.

Chien Wu went to see the eccentric Chieh Yu; the latter asked, "What did Chung Shih tell you some time ago?"

"He told me," said Chien Wu, "that the ruler should set himself as an example, and regulate men with laws and measures. In such a case, none would venture to disobey, and refuse to be transformed."

"That would spoil virtue," said Chieh Yu. "When the ruler tries to get the world in order in this way, he is like wading through the sea, hewing a passage through a river, or making a mosquito carry a mountain on its back. When the sages set the world in order, they have no concern with what is outside human nature. They let every man follow his own proper nature, and go at that. Every man does what he really can do; that is all. The bird flies high to avoid harm from the snare or the dart. The mouse burrows down below the sacrificial place to avoid the danger of being smoked out or dug up. Do you not even know the facts about these two creatures?"

> This story shows that everything has its natural ability. Even the small bird and the little mouse have their natural way of protecting themselves and doing things. The best way to govern is to let things alone and let them act as they can. — *Tr.*

Tien Ken was traveling to the south of Yin Mountain. He had reached the river Liao when he met a nameless sage, to whom he said, "I beg to ask about governing the world."

"Go away," said the nameless man, "you are a low fellow. How unpleasant is your question! I would be in companionship with the Maker of things. When wearied, I would mount on the bird of ease and emptiness, proceed beyond the world, wander in the land of nowhere, and live in the domain of nothingness. Why do you come to worry me with the problem of setting the world in order?"

Tien Ken again asked his question, and the nameless man replied: "Make excursion in pure simplicity. Identify yourself with nondistinction. Follow the nature of things and admit no personal bias, then the world will be in peace."

Yang Tzu Chu went to see Lao Tzu, and said, "Here is a man, alert and vigorous, clearsighted and intelligent, and untiring in learning *Tao*. Could he be accounted a wise ruler?"

"In comparison with the sages," said Lao Tzu, "such a one would be a mere servant or artisan, toiling with their muscles and wearing out their minds. The tiger and the leopard are hunted because of the beauty of their skins. The cleverness of the monkey, the sagacity of the dog, bring them both to the tether. Can such as these be compared with a wise ruler?"

Yang Tzu Chu looked discomposed and said, "May I venture to ask about the government of the wise ruler?"

"In the government of the philosopher-king," said Lao Tzu, "his achievement is the greatest in the world, but it seems not to be his own. His influence reaches all things, but no one depends upon him.

> "The spiritual man has no achievement," as was said in the first chapter. He simply lets every man do his own work according to his own ability. — *Tr.*

"No one can give him a name, but every one enjoys one's self.

> "The sage has no name," as was said in the first chapter. — *Tr.*

"The philosopher-king is he who stands within mystery and makes excursion into the nonexistent."

> "The perfect man has no self," as was said in the first chapter. — *Tr.*

In the state of Cheng, there was a wonderful wizard, named Chi Hsien. He knew all about men's birth and death, gain and loss, misfortune and happiness, long life and short life — predicting the year, the month, and the day, with supernatural accuracy. The people of Cheng used to flee at his approach. Lieh Tzu went to see him and was fascinated. On his return he said to Hu Tzu: "I used to consider your doctrine, my master, as perfect. Now I know something more perfect still."

This story, according to Kuo Hsiang, is to illustrate the different aspects of the perfect man. The perfect man is "tranquil in disturbance," as was said in the last chapter. In other words, he is tranquil in activity. So there are four aspects of the perfect man: (1) tranquillity; (2) activity; (3) the balance of tranquillity and activity; (4) tranquillity in activity. — *Tr.*

"So far I have taught you the literature of my doctrine," said Hu Tzu, "but not its essence. Do you think that you are in possession of it? Without cocks in your poultry yard, what sort of eggs would the hens lay? You displayed your doctrine to the world in order to get credit. That is the reason why this man can interpret your physiognomy. Bring him with you and show me to him."

Next day Lieh Tzu went with Chi Hsien to see Hu Tzu, and when they came out, Chi Hsien said: "Alas! your master is a dead man. He will not live; — not for ten days more! I saw something strange about him. He looked like wet ashes."

Lieh Tzu went in, he wept till the front of his jacket was wet with his tears. Then he told Hu Tzu what the wizard had said. Hu Tzu said: "I showed myself to him in the form of earth. I was naturally immovable like a mountain, [1] though I made no artificial attempt to be immovable. [2] He probably saw me with my natural functions closed up. Try to bring him again."

This is one aspect of the perfect man — tranquillity. — *Tr.*

Next day, accordingly, Lieh Tzu brought the wizard again to see Hu Tzu. When they went out, the wizard said: "It is fortunate for your master that he met me. He is better. He is perfectly alive. I see that the closing up of his natural functions is only temporary."

Lieh Tzu went in and told Hu Tzu. Hu Tzu said: "I

---

1   Reading 萌 as 峚, according to Yu Yueh.
2   Reading 正 as 止, according to Yu Yueh.

showed myself to him in the form of heaven. Fame and real gain do not enter my mind. My natural functions spring forth from the depth of my being. He probably saw me with my natural functions in full activity. Try to bring him again."

This is another aspect of the perfect man — activity. — Tr.

Next day Lieh Tzu came again with the wizard to see Hu Tzu. When they went out, the wizard said: "Your master is never the same. I cannot understand his physiognomy. Wait until he has become normal, and then I will examine him again."

Lieh Tzu went in and told Hu Tzu. Hu Tzu said: "I showed myself to him in the great harmony in which nothing is superior to anything. He probably saw the balance of my natural functions. Where the water whirls about from the swishing of a dugong, there is a whirlpool; where it does so from the checking of its flow, there is a whirlpool; where it does so from onward rushing of its flow, there is a whirlpool. There are nine kinds of whirlpools with different names. I only mentioned three of them. Try to bring him again."

This is another aspect of the perfect man — the balance of tranquillity and activity. The mentality of the perfect man is compared with the whirlpool. Kuo Hsiang said: "By whirlpool Chuang Tzu means the quality of tranquillity and silence. The water has no conscious mind and always follows the nature of things. Therefore, though there is a difference between flowing and checking, between the movement of a dugong and the dance of a dragon, yet the water itself is always silently what it is, and never loses its tranquillity and silence. So is the perfect man. When he is asked to do something, he is active. When he is not asked, he is passive. Though there is a difference between activity and passivity, he is always mysteriously calm. To illustrate this, Chuang Tzu mentioned these different conditions of water. Though there may be the nine different conditions of water, with the confusion of order and disorder, he who is at the height is always simple, enjoys himself, and forgets doing." — Tr.

Next day Lieh Tzu again came with the wizard to see Hu Tzu. But before he had settled himself in his position, the wizard

lost control of himself and ran away.   Hu Tzu said, "Pursue him."
Lieh Tzu did so, but could not catch him.   He returned and told
Hu Tzu: "He disappeared, he is lost.   I could not catch him."

"I showed myself to him," said Hu Tzu, "with change without
losing the essential.   I flexibly follow him with emptiness.   I
do not know who is who, and what is what.   In accordance with
things, I change; in accordance with things, I flow.   Therefore
he ran away."

This is another aspect of the perfect man — activity in tranquillity.
Kuo Hsiang said: "When the perfect man is active, he is like heaven;
when tranquil, he is like earth.   Doing something, he is like the flowing
water; doing nothing, he is like the silent whirlpool.   Though there
is a difference between the flowing water and the silent whirlpool,
between the movement of heaven and the immovability of earth, yet
all these are as they are naturally, not artificially.   Therefore, when
the wizard saw the perfect man sitting and forgetting himself, he thought
that he was going to die.   When he saw the perfect man being active
like heaven, he thought that he was again alive.   In fact, the perfect
man responds to external things with no conscious mind, but mysteriously coincides with reason.   He goes up and down with evolution
and according to the changes of the world.   So he can be the master
of things and can follow time forever.   Therefore, he was not understood by the wizard." — *Tr.*

Upon this Lieh Tzu was convinced that he had not yet acquired any real learning.   He returned to his house; for three
years he did not go out.   He cooked for his wife.   He fed the
pigs as if he were feeding men.

He forgot the distinction between social positions and that between men and animals. — *Tr.*

He had no special predilection for any particular kind of work.

He considered all things as equal. — *Tr.*

He discarded the artificial and reverted to the natural.   He stood
in the world like a clod of earth.   Amidst confusion and disturb-

112

ance, he remained within the One to the last.

Do not be the owner of fame.   Do not be full of plans.   Do not be busy with work.   Do not be the master of knowledge.

Let everything take care of itself. — *Tr.*

Identify yourself with the infinite.   Make excursion into the void.   Exercise fully what you have received from nature, but gain nothing besides.   In one word, be empty.

The mind of the perfect man is like a mirror.   It does not move with things, nor does it anticipate them.   It responds to things, but it does not retain them.   Therefore, he is able to deal successfully with things, but he is not affected by them.

The ruler of the Southern Sea is called Change; the ruler of the Northern Sea is called Uncertainty, and the ruler of the Centre is called Primitivity.   Change and Uncertainty often met on the territory of Primitivity, and being always well treated by him, determined to repay his kindness.   They said: "All men have seven holes for seeing, hearing, eating, and breathing.   Primitivity alone has none of these.   Let us try to bore some for him." So every day they bored one hole; but on the seventh day Primitivity died.

APPENDICES

SOME CHARACTERISTICS OF THE
PHILOSOPHY OF KUO HSIANG

I

Most people have the impression that in the history of Chinese philosophy there was little progress. This impression is created by the fact that most Chinese philosophers were what Chuang Tzu called the "followers of antiquity." When they had ideas, instead of expressing those ideas directly in their own names, they would read them into the sayings of some ancient authority as if they had found them already there. Their writings, therefore, were usually in the form of commentaries. But commentators of this kind were really philosophers; commentaries of this kind were really philosophical works, having intrinsic value in themselves. To this class of commentators and commentaries belonged Kuo Hsiang and his work, "Commentaries on the *Chuang-tzu*." If we realize that Kuo Hsiang was an independent philosopher just as Chuang Tzu had been, we can see that the Taoistic philosophy did not reach its perfection until the sixth century. As a matter of fact, there was progress.

In the history of Western philosophy, philosophers usually expressed their ideas in their own names. A superficial study of history gives people the impression that there were a great variety and great progress. But a careful investigation will show that, variety and progress though there were, they certainly were not so great as they appear to be. William James said that pragmatism is a new name for an old philosophy. To call an old philosophy with a new name is a practice of the philosophers of the West. Philosophers of the East would usually call a new philosophy, when they had one, with an old name. If this practice were also adopted by the Western philosophers; if, for instance, the pragmatists would call themselves nothing more than commentators of Protagoras and their writings the commentaries to the saying: Man is the measure of all things; if Bergson would call himself nothing more than a commentator of Heraclitus and his writings commentaries to the Heraclitean philosophy of change, a superficial observer will also get the impression that in the history of Western philosophy there was little progress. But the fact is that no matter what the pragmatists or Bergson would call themselves, their philosophy has an intrinsic value. I am not denying the fact that in the history of Western philosophy, especially in the modern period, because of the progress of science, there were more progress and variety than in the history of Chinese philosophy. I simply point out that, in either case the progress and variety were not so great or so small as they appear to be.

Some of the important passages of Kuo Hsiang's "Commentaries" I have quoted in the Introduction, and a part of them I translated along with the text of the *Chuang-tzu*. We see that from Chuang Tzu to Kuo Hsiang there was a real development in Taoism. The rough sketch, the poetic suggestions of the former were definitely expressed by the latter in the form of clear and generalized statements. What was an idea in the former became in the latter a well-developed principle. It is needless to say that development is progress. Who can say that there is no progress when a chicken is developed from an egg?

Besides, in Kuo Hsiang's thought, there were really some new points, which, though in perfect harmony with the general spirit of Taoism, were something not said by either Lao Tzu or Chuang Tzu. To summarize these points is the purpose of this Appendix.

2

Lao Tzu and Chuang Tzu denied the existence of God. They thought that in the universe everything just spontaneously produces itself. This idea received full treatment in Kuo Hsiang's

"Commentaries." He emphasized the idea that there is no Creator of things. Fearing that some people might mistake *Tao* as a sort of Creator, he especially emphasized the idea that *Tao* is nothing. When Chuang Tzu said poetically in Chapter VI that *Tao* "causes the gods to be divine and the world to be produced," Kuo Hsiang said:

> "*Tao* is nothing. How can it cause the gods to be divine and the world to be produced? It does not cause the gods to be divine, but they are divine themselves. So *Tao* causes them to be divine by not causing them. *Tao* does not produce the world, but the world produces itself. So *Tao* produces it by not producing it. . . . *Tao* is everywhere, but everywhere it is nothing."

In his commentary to the text of the *Chuang-tzu* in Chapter XXII, Kuo Hsiang said:

> "In existence what is prior to things? We may say that the Yin and Yang are prior to things. But Yin and Yang are themselves things; what is prior to Yin and Yang? We may say that nature is prior to things. But nature is simply the naturalness of things. We may say that *Tao* is prior to things. But *Tao* is nothing. Since it is nothing, how can it be prior to things? We do not know what is prior to things, yet things are continuously produced. This shows that things are spontaneously what they are; there is no Creator of things."

According to Kuo Hsiang, the universe has neither beginning nor end. Being cannot be produced by nonbeing, nor can it pass into nonbeing. In his commentary to the text in the same chapter, he said:

> "Not only that nonbeing cannot become being, being cannot become nonbeing too. Though being may change in thousands of ways, it cannot change itself into nonbeing. Therefore, there is no time when there is no being; being eternally exists."

This theory of being sounds like that of Parmenides.

Kuo Hsiang had other arguments to support the theory

that things spontaneously produce themselves. In his commentary to the text in Chapter XIV, he said:

> "We may claim that we know the causes of certain things. But there is still the question: What is the cause of these cauees? If we continue to ask this question again and again, we have to stop at something that is spontaneously self-produced and is what it is. We cannot ask about the cause of this something. We can only say that it is."

So at last we still have to adopt the theory that things spontaneously produce themselves and are what they are. Since, according to Kuo Hsiang, we have to adopt this theory anyway, why do we not adopt it at the very beginning? If we adopt this theory at the very beginning, we need not ask about the cause of anything. We need not ask the question which is ultimately unanswerable. We can simply say that everything is spontaneously what it is. In his commentary to the text in Chapter II, Kuo Hsiang said:

> "Some people say that the penumbra is produced by the shadow, the shadow by bodily forms, and bodily forms by the Creator. I would like to ask whether the Creator is or is not? If He is not, how can He create things? If He is, He is simply one of the things; how can one thing produce another? ... Therefore, there is no Creator; everything creates itself. Everything produces itself and is not produced by others. This is the normal way of the universe."

3

When Kuo Hsiang said that everything spontaneously produces itself and is what it is, he meant that things are not created by any Creator. He did not mean that among things there are no relations one with another. According to him, there are relations and the relations are necessary. In his commentary to the text in Chapter VI, he said:

> "When a man is born, insignificant though he is, he has the properties that he necessarily has. However trivial his life may be, he

needs the whole universe to be the condition of his existence. All things in the universe, all that exist, cannot cease to exist without having some effect on him. If one condition is lacking, he may not have existed. If one principle is violated, he may not be living."

The idea is that when there are certain conditions or circumstances, certain things are necessarily produced. But they are not produced by any Creator or any individual. In other words, things are produced by conditions in general, not by any other things in particular. Socialism, for instance, is produced when there are certain economic conditions. According to what is known as the materialistic interpretation of history, it was not produced by Marx or Engels, still less by their manifesto. In this sense, we can say: "Everything produces itself and is not produced by others."

If the saying that everything spontaneously produces itself is interpreted in this way, there is no room for free will. In his commentary to the text in Chapter V, Kuo Hsiang said:

"We have our life, not because we wish to have it. Within our life, a span of one hundred years, sitting, rising, walking, standing, acting, resting, gaining, losing, feeling, instinct, knowledge, and ability, all that we have, all that we have not, all that we do, and all that we meet, are so, not because we want them to be so. By natural reason, they are what they are."

In his commentary to the text in the same chapter, he said:

"It is not by accident that we have our life. It is not by chance that our life is what it is. The universe is very extended; things are very numerous. Yet, in it and among them, we are just what we are. Even the universe itself, even the state or the sage, even the most strong or the most wise, cannot be exceptions of this general rule. What we are not, we cannot be. What we are, we cannot but be. What we do not do, we cannot do. What we do, we cannot but do. Let everything be what it is, and then you have peace."

This determinism is applied to social phenomena as well. In his commentary to the text in Chapter VI, he said:

"There is nothing which is not natural.... Peace and disorder, success or failure, ... are all the product of nature, not of man."

By the "product of nature," he meant the necessary result of certain conditions or circumstances. The establishment of the Russian Soviet government, as the socialists would say, was not the achievement of certain individuals, but the necessary result of certain social and economic conditions. In his commentary to the text in Chapter XIV, Kuo Hsiang said:

"The current of history, combined with the contemporary circumstances, is responsible for the present crisis. It is not due to certain individuals. It is due to the world at large. The activity of the sages does not disturb the world, but the world itself becomes disorderly."

4

Kuo Hsiang's theory of being sounds like that of Parmenides. But his philosophy is far more Heraclitean than Parmenidean. He considered the universe as in a flux. In his commentary to the text in Chapter VI, he said:

"Change is a force, unobservable yet most strong. It transports heaven and earth for the new. It carries hills and mountains to quit the old. The old does not stop for a minute, and immediately the new comes. All things change all the while.... All that we meet secretly pass away. We ourselves in the past were not we ourselves now. We ourselves now still have to go with the present. We cannot keep them."

Society is also always in a flux. Human needs change all the while. Institutions and morals which were good in one time may be bad in another. In his commentary to the text in Chapter XIV, Kuo Hsiang said:

"The institutions of the former kings were to meet the need of time. If they continue to exist when time changes, they become bogy

122

to the people, and begin to be artificial."

In his commentary to the text in Chapter IX, he said:

> "Those who imitate the sages imitate what they have done. But what they have done is something already passed, and therefore cannot meet the present situation. It is worthless and should not be imitated. The past is dead while the present is living. If one attempts to handle the living with the dead, one certainly will fail."

In his commentary to the text in Chapter XII, speaking about Shun and King Wu, Kuo Hsiang said:

> "These two sages were to set the world in order when there was a turmoil. One of them did it with peaceful means, while the other by military force. They differed because their time was different. Between them there is no difference of superiority or inferiority."

Society changes with circumstances. When circumstances change, institutions and morals should change with them. If they do not, they become artificial and are "bogy to the people." It is natural that new institutions and new morals will spontaneously produce themselves. The new and the old are different because the time was different. "Among them there is no difference of superiority and inferiority." Kuo Hsiang was not against institutions and morals as such, as Lao Tzu and Chuang Tzu were. He was simply against the institutions and morals that are out of date and therefore artificial.

5

When there is a change of social circumstances, new institutions and morals spontaneously produce themselves. To let them go means to follow the natural. In his commentary to the text in Chapter VI, Kuo Hsiang said:

> "When the water runs down from a high place to a low one, the

current is irresistible. When the small things group with the small, and the large things with the large, the tendency cannot be opposed. When a man is empty and without bias, everything will contribute its wisdom to him. What will he do, who is the leader of men facing these currents and tendencies? He simply trusts the wisdom of time, relies on the necessity of circumstances, and lets the world take care of itself."

That is nonaction. In his commentary to the text in Chapter XI, he said:

"Nonaction does not mean nothing doing. Let everything do what it does, and then its nature will be satisfied."

In his commentary to the text in Chapter XIII, Kuo Hsiang said:

"The carpenter is in nonaction in carving wood, but he is in action in using the ax. The prince is in nonaction in the management of affairs, but he is in action in the control of ministers. The ministers can manage affairs, while the prince can control ministers. The ax can carve the wood, while the carpenter can use the ax. . . . Everything has its office. The high and the low both have their proper places. This is the perfection of the principle of nonaction."

In his commentary to the text in the same chapter, Kuo Hsiang said:

"Comparing the higher rank with the lower, the prince has more leisure and the minister is more busy. Comparing the ancient time with the modern, the affairs in the time of Yao and Shun were simpler and that in the time of Yu and Tang were more complex. But since everything is natural, there is nonaction in every case."

Because of the change of circumstances, the complexity of modern life spontaneously produces itself. It is natural and not artificial. Return to primitivity as expounded by Lao Tzu and Chuang Tzu was what Kuo Hsiang opposed. In his commentary to the text in Chapter IX, he said:

"A good driver must let the horse exercise the full of his ability.

The way to do so is to give him freedom. Some people train the horses with artificial means and use them to an extent beyond their ability. In this way the horses are exhausted and die. If we let the horses do what they can do, compelling neither the slow horse to run fast nor the fast ones to walk on slowly, though we may travel through the whole world with them, they rather enjoy it. Hearing that horses should be set free, some people think that they should be left wild. Hearing the theory of nonaction, some people think that lying is better than walking. These people go too far, and misunderstand Chuang Tzu's philosophy."

Kuo Hsiang had also another interpretation of primitivity and simplicity. In his commentary to the text in Chapter XV, he said:

"If by primitivity we mean the undistorted, the man whose character is not distorted is the most primitive, though he may be capable of doing many things. If by simplicity we mean the unmixed, the form of a dragon and the feature of a phoenix are the most simple, though their beauty is all-surpassing. On the other hand, even the skin of a dog or a goat cannot be primitive and simple, if its natural qualities are distorted by, or mixed with, foreign elements."

6

Lao Tzu and Chuang Tzu opposed sages. In Taoistic literature, the word "sage" has two meanings. By sage the Taoists either mean the perfect man or the man with all sorts of knowledge. Lao Tzu and Chuang Tzu attacked knowledge and sage of the latter kind, the man who has knowledge. From the above quotation, we can see that Kuo Hsiang had no objection to some men's being sages. He had objection only to most people's imitating sages. Plato was born a Plato. Goethe was born a Goethe. Their genius was as natural as the form of a dragon or the feature of a phoenix. They were as primitive and as simple as anything can be. They were not wrong in writing their *Republic* and *Faust*. In doing this they simply followed their own nature. In his commentary to the text in Chapter III, Kuo

Hsiang said:

> "By knowledge we mean the activity that attempts what is beyond one's natural ability; that which does not so is not called knowledge. One should act within the proper sphere of one's natural ability, attempt nothing that is beyond. If one by nature is a strong man, he can carry a very heavy burden without feeling the weight. If one by nature is a skillful man, he can manage all sorts of affairs without feeling busy."

Thus to knowledge Kuo Hsiang gave this special definition. According to him, Plato's *Republic*, Goethe's *Faust*, or even Napoleon's military conquest, were simply the spontaneous expression of their genius, their natural ability. There were no elements of knowledge at all. It is only the imitators that have knowledge. It seems that Kuo Hsiang thought imitation is wrong, for three reasons. First, it is useless. In his commentary to the text in Chapter XIII, Kuo Hsiang said:

> "Events in ancient times have ceased to exist. Though they may be recorded, who can cause them to happen again in the present? The ancient is not in the present, and the present is changing now. Therefore, we should give up imitation, act according to our nature, and change with time. This is the way to perfection."

Since everything is in a flux, the ancient is different from the present, the one is different from the other. Our situations, problems, and needs are changing all the while. Every day we should have new methods to meet our new situations, to solve our new problems, and to satisfy our new needs. Even at the same moment, the situations, problems, and needs of different individuals are also different. So must be their methods. What is the use of imitation?

Second, strict imitation is impossible. One simply must be what one is. In his commentary to the text in Chapter V, Kuo Hsiang said:

> "We have our life, not because we wish to have it. . . . With conscious effort some people try to be great artists, but they can never suc-

126

ceed. Yet without knowing how, the great artists spontaneously become artists. With conscious effort some people try to be sages, but they can never succeed. Yet without knowing how, the sages spontaneously become sages. Not only that the sages and artists are difficult to be imitated, we cannot even be fools, or dogs, by simply wishing and trying to be."

Everything must be what it is. One simply cannot be the other.
Third, imitation is harmful. In his commentary to the text in Chapter II, Kuo Hsiang said:

"There are some people who are not satisfied with their nature, and always attempt what is beyond it. They thus attempt what is impossible. They can never succeed. A circle can never succeed in imitating a square, nor there is any chance for a fish to become a bird. What they try to imitate may be good and beautiful. But the further they go, the more remote their goal seems to be. The more knowledge they gain, the more nature they lose."

In his commentary to the text in Chapter X, Kuo Hsiang said:

"The nature of everything has its limit. If one is induced by what is beyond it, one's nature will be lost. One should disregard the inducement, live according to one's self, but not to others. If so, the integrity of one's nature will be preserved."

There is no possibility for one to succeed in imitating others. But in imitating others, there is a great probability for one to lose one's self. That is the harm of imitation.

If imitation is useless, impossible, and harmful, why should it be there? Why should not every one "live according to one's self, but not to others"? "To live according to one's self" is nonaction.

"To live according to one's self" is the only way for one to be happy. The reason that most people cannot disregard outside inducement is that they do not know the equality of things. They do not know that "from the viewpoint of their sameness, all things are one." Because of this ignorance, they have preferences and prejudices which have no validity in the light of reason.

One must see the oneness of things and identify one's self with it. One who can be so is the perfect man.

7

These are the points which I consider to be the special characteristics of Kuo Hsiang's philosophy. With some of his new concepts, Taoism could be saved from many difficulties. Though his statement is sometimes too formal for practical purposes, he certainly made contributions to Taoism in particular and to philosophy in general.

Though Kuo Hsiang's philosophy, as we see in the above quotations, is more naturalistic and deterministic than that of Lao Tzu and Chuang Tzu, it is no less mystic. This may be seen in the great passages of his "Commentaries," which I translated along with the text of the *Chuang-tzu*. In the combination of naturalism and mysticism lies Kuo Hsiang's greatness.

It is difficult to say how much Kuo Hsiang was influenced by Buddhism. But Kuo Hsiang was a Taoist, anyway. There are several fundamental differences between Buddhism and Taoism. If we are to speak in a most general way, we may say that, while to Buddhism everything is false and wrong, to Taoism everything is real and right. While the metaphysics of Buddhism is idealistic, that of Taoism is realistic. While to Buddhism Nirvana is a metaphysical state, to Taoism the world of pure experience is simply an epistemological one. Therefore Taoism, though having a profound mystic element, has no conflict with science.

There has been a historical problem as to whether Kuo Hsiang's "Commentaries" was really his work. He was accused of being a plagiarist and that his "Commentaries" were the work of Hsiang Hsiu, one of his contemporaries. This accusation, however, is of no importance to us, since our interest is in philosophy, not in history. We can simply consider this accusation as that called by Chuang Tzu "three in the morning" and "follow two courses at once."

THE THIRD PHASE OF TAOISM:
CHUANG TZU

Chuang Chou, better known as Chuang Tzu (c.369-c.286B.C.), is perhaps the greatest of the early Taoists. We know little of his life save that he was a native of the little state of Meng on the border between the present Shantung and Honan provinces, where he lived a hermit's life, but was nevertheless famous for his ideas and writings. It is said that King Wei of Chu, having heard his name, once sent messengers with gifts to invite him to his state, promising to make him chief minister. Chuang Tzu, however, merely laughed and said to them: "... Go away, do not defile me.... I prefer the enjoyment of my own free will."[1]

Chuang Tzu the Man and *Chuang-tzu* the Book

Though Chuang Tzu was a contemporary of Mencius and a friend of Hui Shih, the book titled the *Chuang-tzu*, as we know it today, was probably compiled by Kuo Hsiang, *Chuang-tzu* the book's great commentator of the third century A.D. We are thus not sure which of the chapters of *Chuang-tzu* the book were really written by Chuang Tzu himself. It is, in fact, a collection of various Taoist writings, some of which represent Taoism in its first phase of development, some in its second, and some in its third. It is only those chapters representing the thought of this third climactic phase that can properly be called Chuang Tzu's own philosophy, yet even they may not all have been written by Chuang Tzu himself. For though the name of Chuang Tzu can be taken as representative of the last phase of early Taoism, it is probable that his system of thought was brought to full completion only by his followers. Certain chapters of the *Chuang-tzu*,

---

1 *Historical Records*, Ch. 63.

for example, contain statements about Kung-sun Lung, who certainly lived later than Chuang Tzu.

Way of Achieving Relative Happiness

The first chapter of the *Chuang-tzu*, titled "The Happy Excursion," is a simple text, full of amusing stories. Their underlying idea is that there are varying degrees in the achievement of happiness. A free development of our natures may lead us to a relative kind of happiness; absolute happiness is achieved through higher understanding of the nature of things.

To carry out the first of these requirements, the free development of our nature, we should have a full and free exercise of our natural ability. That ability is our *Te*, which comes directly from the *Tao*. Regarding the *Tao* and *Te*, Chuang Tzu has the same idea as Lao Tzu. For example, he says:

> At the great beginning there was Nonbeing. It had neither being nor name and was that from which came the One. When the One came into existence, there was the One but still no form. When things obtained that by which they came into existence, it was called the *Te*.[1]

Thus our *Te* is what makes us what we are. We are happy when this *Te* or natural ability of ours is fully and freely exercised, that is, when our nature is fully and freely developed.

In connection with this idea of free development, Chuang Tzu makes a contrast between what is of nature and what is of man. He says:

> What is of nature is internal. What is of man is external. . . . That oxen and horses should have four feet is what is of nature. That a halter should be put on a horse's head, or a string through an ox's nose, is what is of man.[2]

Following what is of nature, he maintains, is the source of all hap-

---

1 *Chuang-tzu*, Ch. XII.
2 *Id.*, Ch. XVII.

piness and goodness, while following what is of man is the source of all pain and evil.

Things are different in their nature and their natural ability is also not the same. What they share in common, however, is that they are all equally happy when they have a full and free exercise of their natural ability. In "The Happy Excursion" a story is told of a very large and a small bird. The abilities of the two are entirely different. The one can fly thousands of miles, while the other can hardly reach from one tree to the next. Yet they are both happy when they each do what they are able and like to do. Thus there is no absolute uniformity in the natures of things, nor is there any need for such uniformity. Another chapter of the *Chuang-tzu* tells us:

> The duck's legs are short, but if we try to lengthen them, the duck will feel pain. The crane's legs are long, but if we try to shorten them, the crane will feel grief. Therefore we are not to amputate what is by nature long, nor to lengthen what is by nature short. [1]

Political and Social Philosophy

Such, however, is just what artificiality tries to do. The purpose of all laws, morals, institutions, and governments, is to establish uniformity and suppress difference. The motivation of the people who try to enforce this uniformity may be wholly admirable. When they find something that is good for them, they may be anxious to see that others have it also. This good intention of theirs, however, only makes the situation more tragic. In the *Chuang-tzu* there is a story which says:

> Of old, when a seabird alighted outside the capital of Lu, the Marquis went out to receive it, gave it wine in the temple, and had the *Chiu-shao* music played to amuse it, and a bullock slaughtered to feed it. But the bird was dazed and too timid to eat or drink anything. In three days it was dead. This was treating the bird as one would treat oneself, not the bird as a bird.... Water is life to fish but is death to man. Being differently constituted, their likes and dis-

---

1 *Id.*, Ch. VIII.

likes must necessarily differ. Therefore the early sages did not make abilities and occupations uniform.[1]

When the Marquis treated the bird in a way which he considered the most honourable, he certainly had good intentions. Yet the result was just opposite to what he expected. This is what happens when uniform codes of laws and morals are enforced by government and society upon the individual.

This is why Chuang Tzu violently opposes the idea of governing through the formal machinery of government, and maintains instead that the best way of governing is through non-government. He says:

> I have heard of letting mankind alone, but not of governing mankind. Letting alone springs from the fear that people will pollute their innate nature and set aside their *Te*. When people do not pollute their innate nature and set aside their *Te*, then is there need for the government of mankind?[2]

If one fails to leave people alone, and tries instead to rule them with laws and institutions, the process is like putting a halter around a horse's neck or a string through an ox's nose. It is also like lengthening the legs of the duck or shortening those of the crane. What is natural and spontaneous is changed into something artificial, which is called by Chuang Tzu "overcoming what is of nature by what is of man."[3] Its result can only be misery and unhappiness.

Thus Chuang Tzu and Lao Tzu both advocate government through non-government, but for somewhat different reasons. Lao Tzu emphasizes his general principle that "reversing is the movement of the *Tao*." The more one governs, he argues, the less one achieves the desired result. And Chuang Tzu emphasizes the distinction between what is of nature and what is of man. The more the former is overcome by the latter, the more there

---

1 *Id.*, Ch. XVIII.
2 *Id.*, Ch. XI.
3 *Id.*, Ch. XVII.

will be misery and unhappiness.

Thus far we have only seen Chuang Tzu's way of achieving relative happiness. Such relative happiness is achieved when one simply follows what is natural in oneself. This every man can do. The political and social philosophy of Chuang Tzu aims at achieving precisely such relative happiness for every man. This and nothing more is the most that any political and social philosophy can hope to do.

Emotion and Reason

Relative happiness is relative because it has to depend upon something. It is true that one is happy when one has a full and free exercise of one's natural ability. But there are many ways in which this exercise is obstructed. For instance, there is death which is the end of all human activities. There are diseases which handicap human activities. There is old age which gives man the same trouble. So it is not without reason that the Buddhists consider these as three of the four human miseries, the fourth, according to them, being life itself. Hence, happiness which depends upon the full and free exercise of one's natural ability is a limited and therefore relative happiness.

In the *Chuang-tzu* there are many discussions about the greatest of all disasters that can befall man, death. Fear of death and anxiety about its coming are among the principal sources of human unhappiness. Such fear and anxiety, however, may be diminished if we have a proper understanding of the nature of things. In the *Chuang-tzu* there is a story about the death of Lao Tzu. When Lao Tzu died, his friend Chin Shih, who had come after the death, criticized the violent lamentations of the other mourners, saying:

> This is to violate the principle of nature and to increase the emotion of man, forgetting what we have received [from nature]. These were called by the ancients the penalty of violating the principle of nature. When the Master came, it was because he had the occasion to be born. When he went, he simply followed the natural course. Those who are quiet at the proper occasion and follow the natural course cannot be affected by sorrow or joy. They were considered

133

by the ancients as the men of the gods, who were released from bondage. [1]

To the extent that the other mourners felt sorrow, to that extent they suffered. Their suffering was the "penalty of violating the principle of nature." The mental torture inflicted upon man by his emotions is sometimes just as severe as any physical punishment. But by the use of understanding, man can reduce his emotions. For example, a man of understanding will not be angry when rain prevents him from going out, but a child often will. The reason is that the man possesses greater understanding, with the result that he suffers less disappointment or exasperation than the child who does get angry. As Spinoza has said: "In so far as the mind understands all things are necessary, so far has it greater power over the effects, or suffers less from them." [2] Such, in the words of the Taoists, is "to disperse emotion with reason."

A story about Chuang Tzu himself well illustrates this point. It is said that when Chuang Tzu's wife died, his friend Hui Shih went to condole. To his amazement he found Chuang Tzu sitting on the ground, singing, and on asking him how he could be so unkind to his wife, was told by Chuang Tzu:

> When she had just died, I could not help being affected. Soon, however, I examined the matter from the very beginning. At the very beginning, she was not living, having no form, nor even substance. But somehow or other there was then her substance, then her form, and then her life. Now by a further change, she has died. The whole process is like the sequence of the four seasons, spring, summer, autumn, and winter. While she is thus lying in the great mansion of the universe, for me to go about weeping and wailing would be to proclaim myself ignorant of the natural laws. Therefore I stop. [3]

On this passage the great commentator Kuo Hsiang comments: "When ignorant, he felt sorry. When he understood, he was

---

1 *Id.*, Ch. III.
2 *Ethics*, Pt. 5, Prop. VI.
3 *Chuang-tzu*, Ch. XVIII.

134

no longer affected. This teaches man to disperse emotion with reason." Emotion can be counteracted with reason and understanding. Such was the view of Spinoza and also of the Taoists.

The Taoists maintained that the sage who has a complete understanding of the nature of things, thereby has no emotions. This, however, does not mean that he lacks sensibility. Rather it means that he is not disturbed by the emotions, and enjoys what may be called "the peace of the soul." As Spinoza says:

> The ignorant man is not only agitated by external causes in many ways, and never enjoys true peace in the soul, but lives also ignorant, as it were, both of God and of things, and as soon as he ceases to suffer, ceases also to be. On the other hand, the wise man, in so far as he is considered as such, is scarcely moved in his mind, but, being conscious by a certain eternal necessity of himself, of God, and things, never ceases to be, and always enjoys the peace of the soul. [1]

Thus by his understanding of the nature of things, the sage is no longer affected by the changes of the world. In this way he is not dependent upon external things, and hence his happiness is not limited by them. He may be said to have achieved absolute happiness. Such is one line of Taoist thought, in which there is not a little atmosphere of pessimism and resignation. It is a line which emphasizes the inevitability of natural processes and the fatalistic acquiescence in them by man.

Way of Achieving Absolute Happiness

There is another line of Taoist thought, however, which emphasizes the relativity of the nature of things and the identification of man with the universe. To achieve this identification, man needs knowledge and understanding of still a higher level, and the happiness resulting from this identification is really absolute happiness, as expounded in Chuang Tzu's chapter on "The Happy Excursion."

In this chapter, after describing the happiness of large and small birds, Chuang Tzu adds that among human beings there

---

1 *Ethics*, Pt. 5, Prop. XLII.

was a man named Lieh Tzu who could even ride on the wind. "Among those who have attained happiness," he says, "such a man is rare. Yet although he was able to dispense with walking, he still had to depend upon something." This something was the wind, and since he had to depend upon the wind, his happiness was to that extent relative. Then Chuang Tzu asks:

> But suppose there is one who chariots on the normality of the universe, rides on the transformations of the six elements, and thus makes excursion into the infinite, what has he to depend upon? Therefore it is said that the perfect man has no self; the spiritual man has no achievement; and the true sage has no name. [1]

What is here said by Chuang Tzu describes the man who has achieved absolute happiness. He is the perfect man, the spiritual man, and the true sage. He is absolutely happy, because he transcends the ordinary distinctions of things. He also transcends the distinction between the self and the world, the "me" and the "non-me." Therefore he has no self. He is one with the *Tao*. The *Tao* does nothing and yet there is nothing that is not done. The *Tao* does nothing, and therefore has no achievements. The sage is one with the *Tao* and therefore also has no achievements. He may rule the whole world, but his rule consists of just leaving mankind alone, and letting everyone exercise his own natural ability fully and freely. The *Tao* is nameless and so the sage who is one with the *Tao* is also nameless.

The Finite Point of View

The question that remains is this: How can a person become such a perfect man? To answer it, we must make an analysis of the second chapter of the *Chuang-tzu*, the "Chi Wu Lun," or "On the Equality of Things." In "The Happy Excursion" Chuang Tzu discusses two levels of happiness, and in "the Equality of Things" he discusses two levels of knowledge. Let us start our analysis with the first or lower level. In our chapter on the School of Names, we have said that there is some similarity between

---

1 *Chuang-tzu*, Ch. I.

Hui Shih and Chuang Tzu. Thus in the "Chi Wu Lun," Chuang Tzu discusses knowledge of a lower level which is similar to that found in Hui Shih's ten so-called paradoxes.

The chapter "Chi Wu Lun" begins with a description of the wind. When the wind blows, there are different kinds of sound, each with its own peculiarity. These this chapter calls "the sounds of earth." But in addition there are other sounds that are known as "the sounds of man." The sounds of earth and the sounds of man together constitute "the sounds of Heaven."

The sounds of man consist of the words (*yen*) that are spoken in the human world. They differ from such "sounds of earth" as those caused by the wind, inasmuch as when words are said, they represent human ideas. They represent affirmations and denials, and the opinions that are made by each individual from his own particular finite point of view. Being thus finite, these opinions are necessarily onesided. Yet most men, not knowing that their opinions are based on finite points of view, invariably consider their own opinions as right and those of others as wrong. "The result," as the "Chi Wu Lun" says, "is the affirmations and denials of the Confucianists and Mohists, the one regarding as right what the other regards as wrong, and regarding as wrong what the other regards as right."

When people thus argue each according to his own one-sided view, there is no way either to reach a final conclusion, or to determine which side is really right or really wrong. The "Chi Wu Lun" says: "Suppose that you argue with me. If you beat me, instead of my beating you, are you necessarily right and am I necessarily wrong? Or, if I beat you, and not you me, am I necessarily right and are you necessarily wrong? Is one of us right and the other wrong? Or are both of us right or both of us wrong? Neither you nor I can know, and others are all the more in the dark. Whom shall we ask to produce the right decision? We may ask someone who agrees with you; but since he agrees with you, how can he make the decision? We may ask someone who agrees with me; but since he agrees with me, how can he make the decision? We may ask someone who agrees with both you and me; but since he agrees with both you and me,

137

how can he make the decision? We may ask someone who differs from both you and me; but since he differs from both you and me, how can he make the decision?"

This passage is reminiscent of the manner of argument followed by the School of Names. But whereas the members of that school argue thus in order to contradict the common sense of ordinary people, the purpose of the "Chi Wu Lun" is to contradict the followers of the School of Names. For this school did actually believe that argument could decide what is really right and really wrong.

Chuang Tzu, on the other hand, maintains that concepts of right and wrong are built up by each man on the basis of his own finite point of view. All these views are relative. As the "Chi Wu Lun" says: "When there is life, there is death, and when there is death, there is life. When there is possibility, there is impossibility, and when there is impossibility, there is possibility. Because there is right, there is wrong. Because there is wrong, there is right." Things are ever subject to change and have many aspects. Therefore many views can be held about one and the same thing. Once we say this, we assume that a higher standpoint exists. If we accept this assumption, there is no need to make a decision ourselves about what is right and what is wrong. The argument explains itself.

The Higher Point of View

To accept this premise is to see things from a higher point of view, or, as the "Chi Wu Lun" calls it, to see things "in the light of Heaven." "To see things in the light of Heaven" means to see things from the point of view of that which transcends the finite, which is the *Tao*. It is said in the "Chi Wu Lun":

> The "this" is also "that." The "that" is also "this." The "that" has a system of right and wrong. The "this" also has a system of right and wrong. Is there really a distinction between "that" and "this"? Or is there really no distinction between "that" and "this'? That the "that" and the "this" cease to be opposites is the very essence of *Tao*. Only the essence, an axis as it were, is the centre of the circle

138

responding to the endless changes. The right is an endless change. The wrong is also an endless change. Therefore it is said that there is nothing better than to use the "light."

In other words, the "that" and the "this," in their mutual opposition of right and wrong, are like an endlessly revolving circle. But the man who sees things from the point of view of the *Tao* stands, as it were, at the centre of the circle. He understands all that is going on in the movements of the cricle, but does not himself take part in these movements. This is not owing to his inactivity or resignation, but because he has transcended the finite and sees things from a higher point of view. In the *Chuang-tzu*, the finite point of view is compared with the view of the well-frog. The frog in the well can see only a little sky, and so thinks that the sky is only so big.

From the point of view of the *Tao*, everything is just what it is. It is said in the "Chi Wu Lun":

> The possible is possible. The impossible is impossible. The *Tao* makes things and they are what they are. What are they? They are what they are. What are they not? They are not what they are not. Everything is something and is good for something. There is nothing which is not something or is not good for something. Thus it is that there are roof-slats and pillars, ugliness and beauty, the peculiar and the extraordinary. All these by means of the *Tao* are united and become one.

Although all things differ, they are alike in that they all constitute something and are good for something. They all equally come from the *Tao*. Therefore from the viewpoint of the *Tao*, things, though different, yet are united and become one.

The "Chi Wu Lun" says again:

> To make a distinction is to make some construction. But construction is the same as destruction. For things as a whole there is neither construction nor destruction, but they turn to unity and become one.

For example, when a table is made out of wood, from the viewpoint of that table, this is an act of construction. But from the viewpoint of the wood or the tree, it is one of destruction. Such construction or destruction are so, however, only from a finite point of view. From the viewpoint of the *Tao*, there is neither construction nor destruction. These distinctions are all relative.

The distinction between the "me" and the "non-me" is also relative. From the viewpoint of the *Tao*, the "me" and the "non-me" are also united and become one. The "Chi Wu Lun" says:

> There is nothing larger in the world than the point of a hair, yet Mount Tai is small. There is nothing older than a dead child, yet Peng Tsu [a legendary Chinese Methuselah] had an untimely death. Heaven and Earth and I came into existence together, and all things with me are one.

Here we again have Hui Shih's dictum: "Love all things equally, Heaven and Earth are one body."

Knowledge of the Higher Level

This passage in the "Chi Wu Lun," however, is immediately followed by another statement:

> Since all things are one, what room is there for speech? But since I have already spoken of the one, is this not already speech? One plus speech makes two. Two plus one makes three. Going on from this, even the most skillful reckoner will not be able to reach the end, and how much less able to do so are ordinary people! If proceeding from nothing to something we can reach three, how much further shall we reach, if we proceed from something to something! Let us not proceed. Let us stop here.

It is in this statement that the "Chi Wu Lun" goes a step further than Hui Shih, and begins to discuss a higher kind of knowledge. This higher knowledge is "knowledge which is not knowledge."

What is really "one" can neither be discussed nor even conceived. For as soon as it is thought of and discussed, it becomes something that exists externally to the person who is doing the thinking and speaking. So since its all-embracing unity is thus lost, it is actually not the real "one" at all. Hui Shih said: "The greatest has nothing beyond itself and is called the Great One." By these words he described the Great One very well indeed, yet he remained unaware of the fact that since the Great One has nothing beyond itself, it is impossible either to think or speak of it. For anything that can be thought or spoken of has something beyond itself, namely, the thought and the speaking. The Taoists, on the contrary, realized that the "one" is unthinkable and inexpressible. Thereby, they had a true understanding of the "one" and advanced a step further than did the School of Names.

In the "Chi Wu Lun" it is also said:

> Referring to the right and the wrong, the "being so" and "not being so": if the right is really right, we need not dispute about how it is different from the wrong; if the "being so" is really being so, we need not dispute about how it is different from "not being so". . . . Let us forget life. Let us forget the distinction between right and wrong. Let us take our joy in the realm of the infinite and remain there.

The realm of the infinite is the realm wherein lives the man who has attained to the *Tao*. Such a man not only has knowledge of the "one," but also has actually experienced it. This experience is the experience of living in the realm of the infinite. He has forgotten all the distinctions of things, even those involved in his own life. In his experience there remains only the undifferentiable one, in the midst of which he lives.

Described in poetical language, such a man is he "who chariots on the normality of the universe, rides on the transformations of the six elements, and thus makes excursion into the infinite." He is really the independent man, so his happiness is absolute.

Here we see how Chuang Tzu reached a final resolution of the original problem of the early Taoists. That problem is how to preserve life and avoid harm and danger. But, to the real sage, it ceases to be a problem. As is said in the *Chuang-tzu*:

> The universe is the unity of all things. If we attain this unity

and identify ourselves with it, then the members of our body are but so much dust and dirt, while life and death, end and beginning, are but as the succession of day and night, which cannot disturb our inner peace. How much less shall we be troubled by worldly gain and loss, good-luck and bad-luck![1]

Thus Chuang Tzu solved the original problem of the early Taoists simply by abolishing it. This is really the philosophical way of solving problems. Philosophy gives no information about matters of fact, and so cannot solve any problem in a concrete and physical way. It cannot, for example, help man either to gain longevity or defy death, nor can it help him to gain riches and avoid poverty. What it can do, however, is to give man a point of view, from which he can see that life is no more than death and loss is equal to gain. From the "practical" point of view, philosophy is useless, yet it can give us a point of view which is very useful. To use an expression of the *Chuang-tzu*, this is the "usefulness of the useless."[2]

Spinoza has said that in a certain sense, the wise man "never ceases to be." This is also what Chuang Tzu means. The sage or perfect man is one with the Great One, that is, the universe. Since the universe never ceases to be, therefore the sage also never ceases to be. In the sixth chapter of the *Chuang-tzu*, we read: "A boat may be stored in a creek; a net may be stored in a lake; these may be said to be safe enough. But at midnight a strong man may come and carry them away on his back. The ignorant do not see that no matter how well you store things, smaller ones in larger ones, there will always be a chance for them to be lost. But if you store the universe in the universe, there will be no room left for it to be lost. This is the great truth of things. Therefore the sage makes excursions into that which cannot be lost, and together with it he remains." It is in this sense that the sage never ceases to be.

Methodology of Mysticism

1 *Id.*, Ch. XX.
2 *Id.*, Ch. IV.

In order to be one with the Great One, the sage has to transcend and forget the distinctions between things. The way to do this is to discard knowledge, and is the method used by the Taoists for achieving "sageliness within." The task of knowledge in the ordinary sense is to make distinctions; to know a thing is to know the difference between it and other things. Therefore to discard knowledge means to forget these distinctions. Once all distinctions are forgotten, there remains only the undifferentiable one, which is the great whole. By achieving this condition, the sage may be said to have knowledge of another and higher level, which is called by the Taoists "knowledge which is not knowledge."

In the *Chuang-tzu* there are many passages about the method of forgetting distinctions. In the sixth chapter, for example, a report is given of an imaginary conversation between Confucius and his favourite disciple, Yen Hui. The story reads: "Yen Hui said: 'I have made some progress.' 'What do you mean?' asked Confucius. 'I have forgotten human-heartedness and righteousness,' replied Yen Hui. 'Very well, but that is not enough,' said Confucius. Another day Yen Hui again saw Confucius and said: 'I have made some progress.' 'What do you mean?' asked Confucius. 'I have forgotten rituals and music,' replied Yen Hui. 'Very well, but that is not enough,' said Confucius. Another day Yen Hui again saw Confucius and said: 'I have made some progress.' 'What do you mean?' asked Confucius. 'I sit in forgetfulness,' replied Yen Hui.

"At this Confucius changed countenance and asked: 'What do you mean by sitting in forgetfulness?' To which Yen Hui replied: 'My limbs are nerveless and my intelligence is dimmed. I have abandoned my body and discarded my knowledge. Thus I become one with the Infinite. This is what I mean by sitting in forgetfulness.' Then Confucius said: 'If you have become one with the Infinite, you have no personal likes and dislikes. If you have become one with the Great Evolution [of the universe], you are one who merely follow its changes. If you really have achieved this, I should like to follow your steps.'"

Thus Yen Hui achieved "sageliness within" by discarding knowledge. The result of discarding knowledge is to have no knowledge. But there is a difference between "*having-no* knowledge" and "having *no-knowledge.*" The state of "*having-no* knowledge" is one of original ignorance, whereas that of "having *no-knowledge*" comes only after one has passed through a prior stage of having knowledge. The former is a gift of nature, while the latter is an achievement of the spirit.

Some of the Taoists saw this distinction very clearly. It is significant that they used the word "forget" to express the essential idea of their method. Sages are not persons who remain in a state of original ignorance. They at one time possessed ordinary knowledge and made the usual distinctions, but they since forgot them. The difference between them and the man of original ignorance is as great as that between the courageous man and the man who does not fear simply because he is insensible to fear.

But there were also Taoists, such as the authors of some chapters of the *Chuang-tzu,* who failed to see this difference. They admired the primitive state of society and mind, and compared sages with children and the ignorant. Children and the ignorant have no knowledge and do not make distinctions, so that they both seem to belong to the undifferentiable one. Their belonging to it, however, is entirely unconsciousness. They remain in the undifferentiable one, but they are not conscious of the fact. They are ones who *have-no* knowledge, but not who have *no-knowledge.* It is the latter acquired state of *no-knowledge* that the Taoists call that of the "knowledge which is not knowledge."

INDEX

147